21 RULES OF BLACKNESS

JASON CLUE & SOPHIA NICOLE

authorHOUSE

AuthorHouse™ UK
1663 Liberty Drive
Bloomington, IN 47403 USA
www.authorhouse.co.uk
Phone: UK TFN: 0800 0148641 (Toll Free inside the UK)
UK Local: 02036 956322 (+44 20 3695 6322 from outside the UK)

© 2020 Jason Clue & Sophia Nicole. All rights reserved.

No part of this book may be reproduced, stored in a retrieval system, or transmitted by any means without the written permission of the author.

Published by AuthorHouse 11/24/2020

ISBN: 978-1-6655-8231-5 (sc)
ISBN: 978-1-6655-8230-8 (e)

Print information available on the last page.

Any people depicted in stock imagery provided by Getty Images are models, and such images are being used for illustrative purposes only.
Certain stock imagery © Getty Images.

This book is printed on acid-free paper.

Because of the dynamic nature of the Internet, any web addresses or links contained in this book may have changed since publication and may no longer be valid. The views expressed in this work are solely those of the author and do not necessarily reflect the views of the publisher, and the publisher hereby disclaims any responsibility for them.

Table of Contents

INTRODUCTION xi

1. Know your worth 1

Description 1
The Computer Scientist 2
The Tailor 6
Summary 9

2. Don't force yourself on people 11

Description 11
The Bouncer 12
The Little Black Boy 15
The State of Oregon 17
Summary 19

3. Never underestimate yourself 21

Description 21
Gannibal, the African 22
The Movie Script 26
Summary 28

4. Build on your physical advantages 31

Description 31
The Gym Buff 32
The Track Star 35
Summary 40

5. Don't be a victim 41

Description 41
The Defeatist 43
The Chef 47
Summary 52

6. Eat foods intended for melanin rich people 55

Description 55
The Aunt and Uncle.. 56
The Island Man... 60
Summary 62

7. Acknowledge your connection to Africa ...65

Description 65
The Big Show 66
The Africa Advocate 68
Summary 69

8. Don't sit on the fence....................................71

Description 71
The Athletes 73
The Protest 75
Summary 77

9. Never change teams.....................................79

Description 79
The Flip-flopper 80
The New Neighbourhood.. 82
Summary 84

10. Always celebrate our successes 87

Description 87
The Rapper 88
The Man and His New Car 89
The Hammer.. 92
Summary 94

11. Never speak negatively of black people in front of non-black people 95

Description 95
The Fever 96
The Timekeeper... 98
Summary 100

12. Choose the right partner............................ 101

Description 101
The Chocolate-Vanilla Swirl 103
The Three-Piece Suit 107
The Clubber 111
Summary 114

13. Be an ambassador at all times 117

Description 117
The Ladies' Man... 118
The Office Politics 122
Summary 125

14. Never make excuses for racist behaviour 127

Description 127
The Actor 128
The Groundskeeper 131
Summary 136

15. Discontinue the use of colonial belief systems 139

Description 139
The Master Plan 140
The N Word..143
The Brazilian Grandmother..147
Summary 149

16. Love your hair...151

Description 151
The Baby with the *Good* Hair 153
The Little Black Girl... 156
Summary 159

17. Don't use stereotypes to quantify blackness 163

Description 163
The Brooklynite 165
The Mixed Race Girl 171
Summary 176

18. Take the teachings to the village 177

Description 177
The Rapper 179
The Billionaire 181
The Game Changers... 183
Summary 184

19. Don't hate on the youth 187

Description 187
The Pound Cake 188
The Kid with Big Ideas.. 190
Summary 194

20. Support black businesses and sustain intergenerational wealth 197

Description 197
The Civil War... 198
The Hustler 201
The Sandwich Shop 204
Summary 205

21. Never apologise for your blackness.........207

Description 207
The ATM 208
The Barber's Chair.. 211
The Black Man's New Clothes 213
Summary 215

CONCLUSION 217

Introduction

Firstly, this book is intended to strengthen and unify all people of the African diaspora. The words *black* and *blackness* are simply used as umbrella terms to signify anyone who identifies with African lineage in any part, percentage or whole. These terms are not meant to offend or exclude anyone. You see, to classify us all as just *black* is purposefully reductionist because it breaks us down into that which we all share. It removes the national additives and regional terms like African-American and Afro-Caribbean. By just being *black*, we delineate African lineage but don't need to attach a country as that could be exclusionary, making it necessary to list all the hyphenated Afro + whatevers. Note that we also don't feel the need to use the word *African*, as people born of the continent may feel a stronger connection to that title than those of us born of the diaspora. And let's face it, *black* is just the best term to use. At the end of the day, when have you ever NOT been *black*? Never. Because you're always blackity black, black, black, regardless of where you are born or what the current politically correct saying of the decade used to describe our people may be.

Secondly, the chapters of this book are reactionary, meaning they are the result of our present society. Sadly, this world is riddled with systemic racism that is often so subtle that it goes unnoticed by those participating. In a more perfect existence, there would be no need to list rules for people to follow to achieve the greatness they are clearly capable of – we would just exist and prosper. But as this is not the case, here's our book, filled with both cautionary tales and cheerful triumphs to illustrate each rule we deem necessary. In fact, this list is based both on history and the sum of our personal experiences as people of colour living in the diaspora. These rules are the definition of PRO BLACKNESS and are not ANTI ANYTHING in any way, shape or form. If anyone misconstrues these rules to be ANTI somebody or something, then the true aim of this book has been lost on said person, and ultimately, this book may not be for him or her.

Finally, these rules are not meant to be taken as a personal attack against your current lifestyle or anyone else's. They are merely suggestions as to how we can be stronger as a race of people in the greater context of global citizenry. If you feel personally attacked, please hear us out and understand that the rule is meant to exemplify a pride and standard of excellence in our communities that we aren't all living up to now. We've got a long way to go but start first with this checklist. Which rules do you already subscribe to?

21 Rules of Blackness Checklist

1. ☐ Know your worth
2. ☐ Don't force yourself on people
3. ☐ Never underestimate yourself
4. ☐ Build on your physical advantages
5. ☐ Don't be a victim
6. ☐ Eat foods intended for melanin rich people
7. ☐ Acknowledge your connection to Africa
8. ☐ Don't sit on the fence
9. ☐ Never change teams
10. ☐ Always celebrate our successes
11. ☐ Never speak negatively of black people in front of non-black people
12. ☐ Choose the right partner
13. ☐ Be an ambassador at all times

14. ☐ Never make excuses for racist behaviour
15. ☐ Discontinue the use of colonial belief systems
16. ☐ Love your hair
17. ☐ Don't use stereotypes to quantify blackness
18. ☐ Take the teachings to the village
19. ☐ Don't hate on the youth
20. ☐ Support black business & sustain intergenerational wealth
21. ☐ Never apologise for your blackness

1. Know your worth

"Your crown has been bought and paid for. Put it on your head and wear it."
– Maya Angelou

Description

Even in today's modern society where many of our people are in important positions within large organisations, we are still very much underpaid. The gap between black and white workers is an unwelcomed reality to many of our brothers and sisters. Ironically, the largest disparity is among folks with a bachelor's degree or higher. More school will certainly increase salaries, but education alone is not enough to overcome racial discrimination in pay within the workplace

The Computer Scientist

Ron finished school with a BA in computer science. Upon entering the workplace, he quickly discovered that many of the jobs he applied for required experience. Ron was a methodical person, but he also needed money, so he decided to look for entry-level jobs and work his way up in his chosen company. He quickly found a customer service job in logistics for a mid-sized company. Once Ron mastered his role, he spent the next several months finding out as much as possible about the company, establishing who did what and how they did it. Ron identified ways where he thought the company could benefit and approached his manager with his ideas. Ron was the only person in the whole of the customer service department with a degree and that also included his manager, Lyle. Lyle liked him as he was very conscientious. Naturally, Lyle was more than happy to hear his ideas. Ron pitched an idea for an app which their customers could use to track the movement of their goods in real time. Ron explained that over half of the calls they received were in relation to where and when the customer deliveries would arrive, so by using the app it would reduce customer service calls by fifty percent. The vehicles were already fitted with trackers; thus, the process of syncing it with a tracking system would be relatively easy to achieve. The only real cost would be the development of the computer system itself. Lyle took the proposal to the directors, who loved the idea, and assigned Ron to carry out the task of creating the app. Ron was moved from the customer service team and began work on the new system immediately. In less than six months, he could build a whole new tracking system for the company that was operated through an app. More enticing, the cost of the entire process didn't create any additional expenses for the company.

As you can imagine, the directors were understandably impressed with the new system. Ron was promoted and given a team of three to help manage the tracking system. He was also financially rewarded for his efforts and given a fifty percent pay increase. Ron was clearly happy with what he had achieved in such a short space of time that he never took the time to question his worth. A hefty pay increase and his own team to manage was a fantastic result for someone who was working as a customer service representative only twelve months prior. Ron was now earning a lot more money than the other customer service representatives, but considerably less than the average multimedia programmer. He was even earning less than Lyle, his former manager on the customer service team.

But Ron was happy in his job and newfound responsibilities. He was so pleased that he had no intentions of leaving and stayed at the company for years to follow.

The Tailor

Oliver worked as a tailor in London for many years. After entering a relationship with a woman who lived in a small town 100 miles east of the capital, he decided to follow her there and set up his own business. Oliver was very conscious of the fact that he would be the only black tailor in the whole town as the town was overwhelmingly white. This wasn't something that Oliver was used to having been born and raised in multicultural London. However, he was willing to relocate for love. He also saw the benefits to his career too. As it had been Oliver's lifelong dream to have his own shop, moving to this town made it possible due to the lower business costs compared to that of London. Oliver did have one reservation though and that was how he would be received. He knew he was a good tailor, but would being good be enough to get customers through his door? At the time, the average price of an off-the-rack suit started at around £120, and the price of a bespoke suit (depending on the material) could be anything from £500 to £1000. After some consideration, he decided to open his shop and offered a price of £200 per suit.

Very quickly the customers came, and they were so impressed with the price that instead of just one, they would order two suits. News spread of this talented tailor who was offering such amazing prices for excellent hand-crafted suits. He received so much business that the waiting time for one of his suits was three months. Oliver was working fourteen-hour days on many occasions to try and keep up with the orders. This was also beginning to take a toll on his health. After a conversation with his now wife, they both decided to increase the prices so that they would be more in line with what the other tailors were charging. This then brought the influx of business to a more manageable flow. Oliver wasn't expecting so much work so quickly. And although he was now charging the going rate, which was great, he was already committed to completing over one hundred suits at the ridiculously low price of £200, including materials.

Summary

You were probably taught to be humble and not boast or brag about your talents and accomplishments. This is mostly sound advice because no one wants to make anyone feel inferior or come across as a complete jerk. Yet there is a difference between humbling yourself and appearing lowly or meek. You must never humble yourself so much that you do so at the expense of your worth. Because there are often times when we need to toot our own horn, it is best not to err on the side of caution when it comes to selling ourselves and our skills. Also, we can certainly do this without being total braggarts.

Now, we are a kind and loving people and often want to bless those around us with whatever goods or services we can provide. As we are so good at our crafts, friends and family will undoubtedly want to receive said goods and services. The problem comes when they enter our business world looking for discounts rather than supporting us for what we are worth.

Even worse is when strangers attempt to exploit our good nature because they believe we are ignorant and know no better. Always demanding top price for equal quality when it comes to one's creations, inventions and innovations is a skill that the most successful have already mastered. If we teach our children from young to know their worth and in turn practise what we preach, this issue will no longer afflict our communities.

2. Don't force yourself on people

"You've got to learn to leave the table when love's no longer being served."
– Nina Simone

Description

This is not to be confused or likened to a defeatist attitude nor a notion of anti-inclusive practices. We are pro-inclusion and understand that cooperation with all peoples is important. Therefore, we will continue to collaborate with people of different backgrounds, all whilst striding into previously all-white spaces, knocking down the competition with ease and grace. For the most part, you deserve that seat at the table, sugar. Though, there are some occasions where you should simply accept the fact that whatever it is you think you desired or believed you had to be a part of, you never actually needed in the first place.

The Bouncer

There was a group of young men on a night out on the town. One of the young men was desperate to get into a certain nightclub. This particular club, Knights, was very exclusive, which only made the young man more eager to gain entrance. His friends were more interested in going to the bar across the street, but Nate wasn't hearing what they had to say. He wanted in. Nate convinced the others to try to gain access into Knights too. As they walked towards the door, they all got hyped up as they saw a group of young ladies, scantily dressed, dance their way in. Moving towards the door with big smiles on their faces, Nate was the first to greet the bouncer.

The bouncer eyed him and his friends up and down and promptly stated, "No sneakers allowed." To which his friends shrugged and almost said in unison, "Let's go across the street instead." Nate's response was, "I've got dress shoes in the car." His friends tried to convince him to stick together but being the type of guy that Nate was (he never took no for an answer), they decided to go their separate ways. After changing, Nate returned to the door and the same bouncer looked him up and down again and said, "Sorry, no hats." Nate replied, "That's fine. I'll just put my hat back in the car." He put the hat in the car mumbling to himself, "Why didn't he just say that to start?" But the vision of being inside such an exclusive club provided all the motivation he needed to continue to persuade the security to let him in. He headed back to the door to be met by the same bouncer who had a look of surprise on his face as Nate approached. As Nate started to walk past the man, he was abruptly pulled back. Confused, he looked at the bouncer and said, "I've got dress shoes on and I've put my hat in the car. What else do you want me to do?" The straight-faced bouncer replied, "Yeah, I know. I'm just not letting you in."

The Little Black Boy

In the summer of 2020, a mother was outraged because her son wasn't allowed in a restaurant due to his athletic attire. Yet, there was a white child similarly dressed who was already dining there with his family. When the restaurant employee was confronted with the mother's frustration over the situation, he stood his ground and stated that her child's outfit was against the restaurant's dress code and that the white child's clothes were different. He struggled to convince the mother (and perhaps anyone else) how they were different. Then, he basically said that he didn't get a good look at the white child when he arrived, alluding to the fact that maybe the clothes were similar, but the white child was under the radar when entering the restaurant. After some social media attention (most of the incident was on film), the restaurant went on to change their dress code policy to be more relaxed to appease the outraged masses and address the error in their ways. But here was the problem: the dress code was meant to be exclusionary from its inception. So, removing the ink from the paper did not remove the mentality of the people. The white child waltzed in there unnoticed because the dress code was never created to exclude him.

The State of Oregon

Is this rule still a little foggy? Maybe we need to think bigger than getting into a club or a restaurant. Let's look at one of the majestic north-western states of America, Oregon. Some of you will already know this, so here's a review for you guys. In 1857, the ingenious lawmakers of the territory wanted to ensure that it remained, let's say, uncontaminated. The result? They constitutionalised their whiteness by stating that black people were not allowed to settle there and that this was punishable by law. Keep in mind this was about a decade before slaves were officially freed in the south, so some may have been brought there as slaves whilst others were living there as free men. The lawmakers of Oregon wanted to ensure that none of those blacks would spill over and tarnish their whitewashed existence. They didn't want us there. And they still don't. Although the clause was removed in 1926, linguistically, there were still some racist remnants in their constitution. These remains weren't completely done away with until 2002 when voters decided to remove it and even then, almost 30% voted to keep it in. 30%!

Summary

There are plenty of spaces that we are not welcome and honestly, that's ok. You know why that's ok? Because it's better to know where you stand than to be in the dark about how people really feel about you. We are all for breaking down barriers and believing that we can be whatever we want, and then going on to smash the opposition and achieve great success. Still, there are some circles that will never welcome you no matter how clever you are, how attractive people see you or how much money your bank account houses. You will never fit in. Do not attempt to fit a square peg into a round hole. Just accept the fact that this particular space is not for you and move on to be somewhere and do something bigger than that which does not accept you.

3. Never underestimate yourself

"If my mind can conceive it and my heart can believe it, then I can achieve it."
– Muhammad Ali

Description

We all have that voice that creeps into our heads every now and again which makes us question ourselves and wonder: Can I actually achieve this thing I set out to do? As black people, it seems that we are always having to prove the naysayers wrong by excelling in whatever area we choose to put our minds to. Historically, the odds have often been stacked against us when pursuing our endeavours and on too many occasions we choose to settle for the easier option due to that little voice called self-doubt.

Gannibal, the African

If someone told you that the Russian playwright Alexander Pushkin (who is considered by many to be the founder of modern Russian literature) was the great grandson of a black man from modern day Cameroon, you might be surprised. According to the one drop rule, this would also qualify Alexander Pushkin himself as a member of our brotherhood, but this isn't actually about Comrade Pushkin. We want to talk about his granddaddy. Just who was this black man that found himself in the heart of the Russian Empire in the 1700s? Abram Petrovich (also known as Gannibal) is believed to have been born in present-day Cameroon in the late seventeenth century. He was kidnapped as a child, taken to Russia and presented to Peter the Great as a gift. The idea was for the young Abram to carry out menial duties within the palace and to be a novelty piece when important guests from Europe would visit. Shocking those in the court, within a very short space of time, Abram learned quite a bit and was fluent in Russian. The Tsar liked the young boy due to his high IQ and very soon he was adopted and raised in the emperor's court as his godson. Abram would accompany the emperor on his military crusades where the young man would serve as his personal assistant.

When he was in his early twenties, he went on to the city of Metz to obtain an education from one of the most distinguished institutes in Europe. By then, he had outshined his peers in mathematics and was also multilingual. With the intention of impressing his godfather, he joined the French Army the next year. At this time, France and Spain were at war. Abram joined on France's side, working his way up to become a captain. Following this victory, the now mature Abram took on the moniker Gannibal out of immense respect for Hannibal, the great Carthaginian general.

Returning to Russia the year after, Gannibal worked as an engineer and then as an instructor in mathematics. When Peter the Great died in 1725, Prince Menshikov became ruler of Russia. Menshikov did not like Gannibal and was distrustful of his non-Russian background, perhaps even intimidated by the African's superior education. Gannibal was banished to the far corners of Siberia in 1727 in the hope that the region's harsh conditions would prove too challenging. Gannibal didn't just complete his service in Siberia, but during this time he also headed many construction projects, one of which was the creation of a fortress leading to his title of master engineer.

When Elizabeth of Russia took the throne in 1741, she appointed Gannibal to her court. During this time, he moved up the ranks again to become a major-general and was titled superintendent of Reval. The following year, the Empress Elizabeth gave him the Mikhailovskoye estate in the northwest of the country with a bevy of servants who worked and lived on the land. Abram Gannibal Petrovich fathered ten children, including a son, who in turn would have a daughter, Nadezhda. Nadezhda was mother to Alexander Pushkin, the one considered by many as the greatest Russian poet of all time.

The Movie Script

As Myles finished reading the script, the producers sat waiting for his response. The movie premise was that aliens (pretending to be humans) ran a hotel. It centred around six random hotel guests who discover that the hotel was just a front for the headquarters of an alien invasion. The guests work together to defeat the aliens and prevent the world from being taken over.

The producers stared intently at Myles and one finally spoke, "We really want you on board for this project. What are your first thoughts?" Myles paused and then spoke, "Yeah, it's interesting, I can see how it could work." The other producer responded, "Which hotel guest do you see yourself playing?" Myles replied, "I like the role of Kurt." The casting director interjected, "Myles, when my colleague said which hotel guest do you want to play, he was referring to one of the African-American characters." Myles smiled before responding, "Ok, here's the issue – you have six hotel guests, three white and three black. The white characters are a professor, scientist and a detective. Then we have the black characters who consist of a drug dealer, pimp and an escaped prison convict. Can you see why I am not interested in the *black* roles?" One of the producers responded, "Well, what do you suggest then?" Myles replied without hesitation, "Just switch the roles up." The casting director answered, "We can't do that. It's just not realistic." Myles replied, "So a movie about aliens managing a hotel suddenly becomes unrealistic when you have a black scientist?"

Summary

While it is true that we don't all begin at the same starting point, we all do possess the ability for self-improvement. It would be silly to make a statement like *we can all achieve greatness* because greatness can be defined in so many ways. One thing is for sure is that we can achieve greater than what we are currently achieving as there is always room for self-development. What we mustn't do is look at what someone else is doing that appears difficult and believe that the only reason they can do it well is because they are better than us. They have only achieved success because they have mastered that particular thing, likely from practice. Where we begin in life is out of our hands, but we can choose our destination, so let's not allow outside influences direct our path to the one that does not benefit us.

In a society where we often find ourselves at a social disadvantage, we can sometimes play into a role that was created for us. You often hear black actors complaining about the roles that they are being cast for: gang bangers, pimps, or other types of ratchet characters. In that situation, someone is writing the script and the actor can choose whether to accept or decline the role. Life is no different – you can reject or accept the role which society is trying to direct you in. Neither your surroundings nor your current situation should dictate your behaviour; however, this is easier said than done. We do not always know the qualities that we have and on many occasions, it takes someone to see in us what we don't always see in ourselves.

4. Build on your physical advantages

"I was built this way for a reason,
so I'm going to use it."
— Simone Biles

Description

There are physical differences amongst the various races of people around the world and as African descendants we have many attributes which are exclusive to us. Whether it be a greater fat-free body mass, the ability to build muscle at an exceptionally fast rate, an increased amount of collagen in our skin (which results in the noticeable delay of the visible signs of ageing), a higher percentage of fast twitch fibres, or more of the slow twitch variety (which support long distance endurance activities), we are at a significant physical advantage.

The Gym Buff

Aaron was a skinny teenaged kid of Caribbean descent who was never very good at sports. He grew up in a predominantly white neighbourhood in a provincial town in the middle of England. He always felt he didn't fit the racial stereotype of being athletically gifted. He was never particularly fast at running and sucked at the sports which were played at school. However, he was very intelligent, so very early on in his life he resided to the fact that he was brains not brawn just as many people subscribe to the belief that you can't be both. He continued this thinking well into his late twenties.

At this point, he was comfortable in his career and on the dating scene. Though his long-time friend, Stuart, started going to the gym with the intention of gaining some muscle (he thought it would increase his chances in the dating game). Stuart too was what would be considered by most people a nerd and he had designs of changing his image. Stuart constantly nagged Aaron to join the gym so that he would have a training partner. After a few months, Stuart finally wore him down and Aaron agreed to take out a membership. They went three times a week mixing cardio and weights in their routine. Within a couple of months, Aaron had already caught Stuart up in terms of strength and was making noticeable gains. They both got the gym bug big time and decided to increase their visits from three times a week to five times a week. Stuart decided to totally change his diet and include meal supplements too, but Aaron felt he was making enough progress without having to change anything. By the end of the year, Aaron's body had completely transformed from a guy who looked like he needed a sandwich to that of an Olympic boxer. This was achieved in less than twelve months. Stuart also made progress but hadn't seen the types of changes that Aaron had experienced. Aaron's body responded faster to the training than Stuart's, hence why he saw much quicker results.

The Track Star

Ayeesha was in her first year of university with a full-fledged four-year plan to conquer the campus and then the world. She was a striking eighteen-year-old girl with velvety smooth brown skin, a slim but curvy hour-glass figure and kinky coils that danced around her afro as she walked. Her mother insisted that she never relax it straight so when it wasn't out in a 'fro, she had it in two neat cornrows to keep it out of her face. Her lips were full, her nose was as cute as a button and her big brown, almond-shaped eyes had always captured her daddy's heart. Ayeesha had been told that she was gorgeous from day one by her two doting parents and two sets of grandparents, not to mention a boy or two around the neighbourhood. Yet Ayeesha never really paid them any mind. For she was also a track athlete, with muscles to adorn her curves and had never had any time for flattery and foolishness, or even many friends for that matter. In college, between the rigours of university coursework and her coach's demanding track practice schedule, she pretty much always stayed busy.

But who wants to spend all their time with no play and all work? Ayeesha made a little break in her timetable to hang out with two girls she had met in her Thursday morning psychology class, Lydia and Nina. These two brown-skinned beauties were the only other ladies of colour in the class. Lydia, with the 8A Brazilian straight locks, and Nina, with a permanently-pressed bleached blonde bob, were fairly smart young ladies with lofty goals. But they lacked depth. You see these girls tended to graze all day with salads and cereal bars (when they weren't on some juice-inspired cleanse). As their diets were never consistent, they peppered these salad days with ultimate junk food binge sessions, consuming food amounting to that of a six-person family. Although they had a similar build to Ayeesha, it was partially hidden by a bit of puppy fat on their faces and around the mid-section because the only exercise they got was walking to and from classes.

Despite their differences, the trio hit it off from the start whilst quietly giggling at their goofy professor and only deepened their bond as they commiserated over a cram session to pass a midterm worth fifty percent of their grade. During this time, Ayeesha heard the girls' complaints that their curves were too curvy, and they wished they didn't have such big backsides. She was puzzled at how much these two fussed over their so-called imperfections. She couldn't make sense of their lack of true self love, especially when they didn't seem to be proactive in getting themselves in better shape. Although Nina and Lydia seemed a bit vapid and self-sabotaging at times, Ayeesha felt it her mission to rid them of their self-hatred. By January, she capitalised on the whole *new year, new me* attitude and told the girls she was going to help them get their bodies back into the shape they were born to have. She started them off slowly by doing a light jog around the neighbouring park just off campus. The two ladies were reluctant to come back for another session, but Ayeesha somehow convinced them to keep at it if they wanted to see results. After jogging every other day for a week, she added some muscle training to their routine and took them to the university's gym. She also introduced them to healthy meal plans that her coaches had been showing her for years. Resisting at every turn, the girls were reminded that this was their resolution and they all stuck with it well into February. Sadly though, Lydia found a new beau just before Valentine's Day and fell off the wagon, citing lack of time as her excuse for missing the workouts. However, Nina was committed to the plan. By summer, her swimsuit hugged onto every perfectly sculpted curve, while Lydia was still rocking a cover-up. She was also newly-single as the relationship from February didn't have the longevity she had hoped for. Ayeesha hadn't given up on her yet so when she heard her admiring her friends' fit bodies, she encouraged her to come back to the gym with them. Lydia just brushed off her invitation and said, "Girl, that's just not for me."

Summary

Although we come in all shapes and sizes, one thing that scientists agree on is that our bodies have a greater propensity to build muscle and burn fat than all other racial groups. We don't all have to look like Black Panther or Storm from X-men, but we definitely can look like the best versions of ourselves. We have the genetics to do it easier than most so why waste what we have been blessed with? Make the most of what we have been given.

5. Don't be a victim

"Nobody can give you freedom. Nobody can give you equality or justice or anything. If you're a man, you take it."
– Malcolm X

Description

Sometimes the odds just don't seem in your favour. We get it – maybe no one in your family has been to university, maybe your mother and father were quite young when they had you so they grew up alongside you or maybe you were raised in a single parent household and didn't get to see much of that lone parent because he or she worked too much. Maybe you're still feeling the ill effects of some generational-curse-type-cycle of poverty that no one in your family could break free from because the system has been rigged against your kinfolk. Sometimes life just is not fair. Sometimes those born with the silver spoon don't take advantage of half the opportunities those born without would jump on. So what though. Yeah. So. What. These are still not good enough excuses to choose a path of victimhood. While it's acceptable to recognise that you may not have had it as easy as others, you cannot allow your misfortunes to decide your fate.

The Defeatist

Growing up on a public housing development in New Orleans, Calvin was already at a social disadvantage. By the age of twenty-three Calvin had already gone to jail, been shot, got caught up in substance abuse issues and fathered a child. Calvin had never been able to hold down a job for more than two months. He also wasn't with the mother of his child and was unable to provide any type of financial support for his kid due to his unstable situation. Calvin is what some people would call a first class screw up, but Calvin didn't see himself like that.

Calvin always believed it was someone else's fault. The time he went to jail he was offered a plea deal. He didn't actually do the robbery, but he followed his lawyer's recommendations by not taking it to trial and did three years instead. When he was shot, it was because he was with his friend who had badly beaten up a guy a week prior. The guy's older brothers ran up on them as they were outside a corner store. His friend died of his wounds, but Calvin recovered. Witnessing the death of his best friend made Calvin turn to drugs. It was around this time when Calvin met Trish. They both were hanging out at a local dealer's house when they took a liking to each other. Not long into the relationship, Trish got pregnant and immediately decided to turn her life around. She stopped drinking and smoking and urged Calvin to do the same. Calvin insisted that he didn't want to be a father and suggested that she get an abortion. Trish wasn't listening and told Calvin that she would be having the baby with or without him. Trish pushed Calvin into finding work, but being an ex-convict meant that the only companies that were willing to take him on were paying what he considered peanuts. Calvin bounced from job to job – one month he was washing dishes in a restaurant, the following month he was unloading boxes. Each time he would end up in an argument with the boss or a patron and find himself without a job. Trish finally gave up on him a few weeks before the baby was born, and the two went their separate ways. Calvin had a brother who was eighteen months younger – he was a standout basketball player, so managed to get a college scholarship. Ironically he wasn't nearly as talented as his older brother Calvin, yet he went off to study at Florida State University. He eventually settled in Atlanta, got married, had a couple of children and managed a successful real estate company. For Calvin's fortieth birthday, his brother invited him to celebrate it over at his house in Atlanta as a way of getting the family together. As the night drew to a close, his fourteen-year-old nephew, noticing the difference between the two siblings, asked Calvin a thought-provoking question. He asked, "Uncle, how is it that your life and dad's life turned out so different?" Without a moment's hesitation Calvin answered, "I've just had bad luck all my life. My lawyer screwed me over when I was not much older than you, which meant that I did time. When I got out, my best friend was involved in some BS which almost got me killed. Another friend of mine got me into smoking, because before that I didn't even drink. Then you got Tyron's mother. She was a real piece of work, caused me so much stress and then stopped me from seeing my son. And you know when you've got a record nobody wants to employ you, so you can't ever get a job. Then, the times when I have got a job that female tries to claim backdated child support. It's tough out here for a brother. The man doesn't want to see us rise up.

The Chef

It was 6:30 in the evening and Ebony was exhausted. Her two kids, Noah aged eight and Ava aged twelve, were doing their homework at the dining room table as she stared into the fridge hoping the ingredients for dinner would leap out onto the stove and fix themselves. Ebony was tired. Like really tired. And fed up. She was twenty-seven years old, raising two kids on her own and working as a cook at a local run-of-the-mill, family-themed chain restaurant. She had just finished a ten-hour shift that spanned across breakfast, lunch and happy hour with demanding wait staff desperate to get their orders out faster than she could cook them. At this point, she wished she had brought home some of the lunchtime leftovers to warm up and serve to her kids. Alas, there were no leftovers, so she quickly rustled up a chicken and rice dish, coupled with a few slices of avocado on the side. Noah, the first to finish, practically inhaled his last bite and gleaned at his mother, "You cook so good, mama. You should just open up your own restaurant." Ebony, tickled at the thought of being an entrepreneur, chuckled and said, "That's a nice idea, but I am not sure where I'd get the money to start it." Ava chimed in and asserted, "Noah's right. Your food is always on point." Ebony, still tired, said, "Yes, baby. I know I'm a good cook, but people like me don't open restaurants. Having your own restaurant is a lot of hard work."

"Uh, mama, when have you ever been afraid of a little hard work?" Ava questioned.

Ebony just smiled back at her baby girl. That night she thought about what she said: *when have you ever been afraid of a little hard work?* Her whole life had been hard work. She didn't talk about how tired she was or how stressed out she got at being the sole provider for her kids. She just did what she had to do, often with a smile on her face. Her kids knew that about her. They knew that she wasn't a complainer. She always made it work, made every penny stretch and ensured that they were taken care of, even if she went without. But was that enough? She wanted them to see her as successful too, not just someone who got by. She decided to do some research into what it takes to have your own restaurant. It required a lot of money and she thought that her credit history probably wouldn't allow for a business loan. That's when Ebony decided the best way to start would be to sell plates of food from her house.

It was an easy sell. She advertised her food on social media where she already had hundreds of friends, many of whom were already fans of her cooking. Starting off little by little, she designated one of her days off each week to create food orders. She drummed up business by posting pictures of previous dinners she'd made for her kids with polls asking people to vote on which foods they'd like to see the following week. Gradually, she built a business that was not just funded by friends and family, but by friends of friends through word of mouth. Soon, people were asking her to cater their weddings, baby showers and quinces. All this was done in the modest kitchen of her three-bedroom townhouse. Eventually, she had saved enough money to take her business outside of her home and rent a space not too far from her house. She continued the catering services and operated mostly as a takeaway service from the location with just a couple of tables and chairs for the occasional patrons who dined in. A few years had passed, and that location had done so well that she opened up another on the other side of town. Ava, sixteen and driving now, stopped by the second location as Ebony was doing some last-minute alterations before the grand opening the following day. As she walked in, Ava smiled at her mother and said, "Imagine if you had been afraid of a little hard work, mama. You'd never have accomplished this much. I'm so proud of you."

Summary

Nobody is suggesting that we forget hundreds of years of oppressive acts that have lynched our fathers, raped our mothers and all but depleted our indigenous lands of their resources. All of that happened. And then some. It is inarguably these practices that have altered our own self-image and dehumanised us in front of a world stage, making many of us feel inferior as a race. The problem is, if we focus on that which doesn't serve us, we fall victim to ignoring that which benefits us. If all you can draw from is your negative history, you subconsciously walk around with a chip on your shoulder that may block blessings. While we must not forget what has happened to us, we must also remember our triumphs outside of this race struggle. We must teach our children how we continually thrive with expertise in the arts, sciences and sports, to name a few.

A victim mentality will never benefit us as a people because the main focus is not on progress. Being a victim is counterproductive to our advancement. Because victims are never responsible for anything that happens to them. They are neither at fault nor can be held accountable for their actions. A victim is not in charge of their destiny; they therefore put all the power in the hands of their oppressor, something we simply cannot afford to do.

6. Eat foods intended for melanin rich people

"Real *Soul Food* is food that enhances the soul, our central sun, our melanin, our carbon, fruits, vegetables, grains; this is real *Soul Food*."
— Dr Sebi

Description

You may be familiar with the expression *eat to live*. This particular phrase rings true, especially when talking about our people. Basically, it's all about eating food that sustains a healthy body and life. A phrase you may not be familiar with is *eat to die*, which is also relevant today. Many of our people are eating the wrong types of food. This can lead to a poor quality of life and in many cases, premature death. We need to ensure that the food we consume is of the highest quality and engineered specifically for our melanin rich bodies.

The Aunt and Uncle

We all know a friend or family member who did not make it to the ripe old age they should have due to complications from a preventable disease like type two diabetes, high blood pressure, etc. Let's take a look at a family you may already be familiar with. They may even be your own:

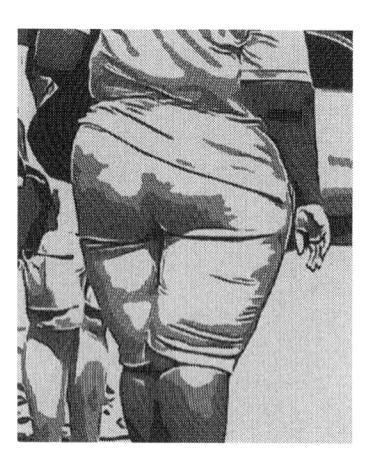

Aunt Sonya and Uncle Mike both worked full time and have two kids. They were not broke, just middle class. They could afford a modest yet comfortable home, two cars, annual vacations, extra tuition for the kids and even overpriced sneakers. Aunt Sonya worked at a supermarket and Uncle Mike was a manager at a car rental place. They loved each other. They loved their kids. But they didn't show their bodies any love. Aunt Sonya and Uncle Mike lead full lives. They each worked at least forty hours a week and kept their kids involved in all kinds of activities from football practice to gymnastics almost every weekend.

Aunt Sonya oversaw meal preparations and she did her best to stock the fridge with foods she knew her kids would eat. She kept frozen broccoli and corn in the freezer too to quickly add some vegetables to meals at the last minute. In between being the kids' chauffer and working her butt off, she inadvertently cut a lot of corners in the family's diet. She liked a bargain, so she would buy big packs of hot dogs when they were on sale. She liked to keep the kids happy, so she bought *juice* (read: coloured, artificially flavoured sugary drinks) by the gallon. She especially liked to keep her husband happy, so when she found the time to cook from scratch, you better believe she fried up some chicken and accompanied it with the richest macaroni and cheese, the kind you can feel clogging your arteries as you eat it, but it tastes soooo good. When she had no time to put in the work in the kitchen, she found her bargains on the dollar menu at pretty much any fast food restaurant en route to whatever activity was on the agenda for that day. She justified the $3-$4/person price tag because it was quick and even better, it was such a good deal, right?

Sadly, Aunt Sonya died at the age of 56 from complications due to her diabetes. Uncle Mike followed her just a few years later with a fatal heart attack. And the two beautiful kids are now in their thirties with kids of their own, but they don't participate in those activities that they did as kids because Aunt Sonya and Uncle Mike only shuttled them around to sporting events; they never actually demonstrated a love for exercise themselves. As a result, Aunt Sonya and Uncle Mike's children grow up to become obese and the grandchildren are on their way to the same fate.

The Island Man

Whenever anybody met Moses, they always just assumed he was a fit and healthy forty-something, the kind who goes for runs each day with his personal trainer and attends the spa three times a week for facials and other beauty treatments. Moses moved to Miami from Jamaica when he was already a grown man with adult children. Truth be told, Moses was sixty-two years old and although active, he had never seen the inside of a gym in his life. He got his exercise from maintaining his garden and walking each day.

People often asked Moses if he had found the fountain of youth, but for Moses it was very simple, he ate to live. He consumed the traditional food that had been passed down through the generations. Fortunately for our Caribbean brothers and sisters, their diet has historically been better than the African-American mainly due to the ability to grow similar foods which were eaten back on the continent of Africa.

Summary

This book is not meant to be some kind of healthy-living guide for life with a calorie-counting meal plan for black folks. The intention of the book is to be an all-around guide to living your best black life. Unfortunately, many of us aren't doing that with the foods we consume. The main issue for folks like African-Americans, for example, is that we have been conditioned to believe that soul food is the food intended for us because we make it taste so darn good. The truth is, we adapted the scraps given to us as slaves and made yummy meals out of them; this tradition remains strong today. What we must not forget is that those foods began as scraps, and no matter how much of grandma's special seasonings we add or how deep in oil we fry it, that food is killing us. We were not meant to consume so much grease. Combine this with the unwavering marketing of unhealthy processed foods of the twenty first century that seem ever persistent in many of our lower income neighbourhoods, and it's a recipe for death.

Our bodies and brains work at optimal performance when we fuel them with good, old-fashioned whole foods — fruits and vegetables that grow in the climates we originated from like yam, mango, ochre, etc. Now this doesn't mean we all need to turn raw vegans. We just need to be more mindful that salt intake combined with sugary and fatty foods have led to many of our people's deaths, and we cannot subscribe to this deadly meal plan any longer.

7. Acknowledge your connection to Africa

"A people without knowledge of
their past history, origin and culture
is like a tree without roots."
– Marcus Garvey

Description

There is a large portion of the African diaspora that have often distanced themselves from anything associated with Africa, instead choosing to affiliate themselves with the land in which they were born. There is nothing wrong with having national pride, but not having any racial pride is what keeps our people disconnected. The image of Africa that the media like to project is usually one of extreme poverty, simplicity and hopelessness. It is no surprise that people are not making the effort to be connected with it.

The Big Show

Live Aid was a music-based fundraising event which was designed to assist with famine relief in Africa. Now we can debate whether the extravaganza had any real impact on the poor people of that region. However, one thing is for sure was the impact it had on the African diaspora when seeing that starving child with flies on her face, which was played on every news outlet on a loop.

All that did was reinforce the existing belief that Africa was not a place we wanted any affiliation to. Then we move on to education, just how is the African depicted in schools to young impressionable children? Usually you will see a tribesman with a shield and spear in the African savannah. Nothing wrong with that image, right? But when you're shown the European, they would show you King Louis XIV, in all his opulent glory.

It is no coincidence that the continent is constantly portrayed as a place to be avoided. Paradoxically, Africa is the richest continent in the world in terms of its natural resources, so clearly somebody must like going there. The same media outlets that keep telling us to help but discourages us to go and see for ourselves are run my corporations who exploit the people of the continent and bleed the water out of the well. Africa is the cradle of civilisation with a rich history and beautiful scenery. Since the invention of the internet, we do not have to rely on television and newspapers to be spoon-fed a version of Africa. Now we can type into a search engine the affluent areas of cities in Nigeria, Angola and many more to see for ourselves, but you might be surprised that you will not find a kid with flies on their face anywhere in sight.

The Africa Advocate

Marcus Garvey, born on the island of Jamaica in 1887, was inspired by the writings of Edward Wilmot Blyden, one of the early pioneers of the Pan-African movement. Garvey sought to unify and connect people of African descent worldwide.

He visualised a world in which black people owned farms, printed newspapers, operated factories and controlled shipping companies. Garvey didn't distance himself from Africa, but instead associated himself with every aspect of it. Garvey was aware of the rich history throughout the continent. This filled him with a strong sense of pride. He understood that for black people to truly unite, they first had to identify with Africa.

Summary

Growing up in the nineties in the USA, terms like *African booty scratcher* and *fresh off the boat* were used to refer to anyone who had newly migrated to the United States from an island nation or the African continent. The offspring of these newcomers were often teased for their *green* status with any similarities in culture being dismissed because we were taught that they were different. Foreign. As an adult, it seems absurd that we may have engaged in such xenophobia. Psychologically, I guess you could explain it away. Maybe we felt a touch of inferiority based on our own status as African-Americans, and in an effort to not be the last man on the totem pole, we lashed out at whoever seemed like easy prey. That kid with the funny accent, the one over there with the non-designer sneakers, anyone whose mother turned up at the school in traditional garb— these kids were easy targets. What we failed to realise was just how alike we were to these *foreigners*. On the surface, we weren't the same at all. But dig a little deeper and it's quite evident that from our foods, dance moves, music and the way our parents disciplined us, we were far more alike to the newbies than we'd ever actually admit to our white peers. As grown-ups, this kind of stuff is obvious: the African diaspora is connected to the motherland because, duh, it's where we originate. So, instead of letting non-Africans carve up and capitalise the continent, we must wholeheartedly embrace our roots. Alongside our African brothers and sisters, let's invest our time, money and energy into the motherland.

8. Don't sit on the fence

"In the end, we will remember
not the words of our enemies, but
the silence of our friends."
– Martin Luther King, Jr.

Description

Within the United States, Great Britain and pockets of Western Europe, the biracial population is very much on the increase and showing no signs of slowing down. One begs the questions: When an interracial couple decide to start a family, how much thought is given to the conflict that the child will find themselves in as they reach maturity? Many parents will take the idealistic approach and tell the child that they are both black and white or that colour is not important, but at some point, they will find themselves in a situation where they will undoubtedly feel more one colour than the other. Then there are occasions when someone has two black parents yet have identity issues which would be more in line with what you might expect a biracial black person to undergo. The fact of the matter is whether you have one black parent or two black parents, educated or uneducated, raised in poverty or born into money, your experience in society will fundamentally be the same.

The Athletes

When asked by a reporter to provide a black perspective on a topic, O.J Simpson said the now infamous words, "Well, I'm not black. I'm O.J." He was not the first superstar athlete to deliver that same sentiment when asked to give a *black* point of view. Twenty years prior in the 1960s, Brazilian soccer superstar Edson Arantes do Nascimento, otherwise known as Pele, was asked what it was like for a black man visiting foreign countries in Europe and Asia. Pele answered the question like many superstars do by referring to themselves in the third person. He stated, "Pele has no colour, Pele goes to Russia and he's treated like a Russian, Pele goes to Germany and is treated like a German, you see

Pele has no colour." There have been many stars within sports and entertainment who have said similar things over the years. Celebrities can be forgiven to a certain degree because whilst at the height of their fame they could be fooled into thinking that they are in fact colourless. For example, O.J. may have believed what he said at the time, but he sure found out that his statement wasn't accurate when he was on trial for murdering his wife.

The Protest

Richard would dread going into work the day after there was some civil unrest because he always knew what was coming. The moment he went into the kitchen to make his coffee, he'd be hit with something along the lines of, "Hey Rich, how 'bout that police killing that kid or choking that man or shooting that woman while she was sleeping in her bed – honestly, insert any of these actual scenarios in – Do you think it was an accident?"

In the most recent incident, Richard just shrugged his shoulders and continued to make his drink, "I don't know. I haven't been following the news." Richard just hated those topics. He had spent his whole life trying to fit in. He was raised by his white mother and white stepdad. Richard had never met his biological father and had no contact with that side of his family. Whenever the matter of race was mentioned, he would do everything possible to avoid the subject. As Richard was leaving the kitchen, he was stopped by one of his colleagues, "So I guess you'll be out protesting tonight then," said the man. Richard was at boiling point by then and snapped at his co-worker, "Why would you think that I have nothing better to do than to be out protesting?" The man made a confused expression before responding, "I'm going, and I assumed you'd be going too."

Summary

Plenty of people go through life without ever ruffling any feathers. They don't like to engage in controversy and tend to avoid conflict, even at the expense of hiding how they really feel about certain issues. That's fine for those people. We are not those people. We are not afforded such luxuries as being able to sit on the fence when it comes to race relations. In theory, a colour-blind society is not a bad thing. There are some idealists that believe we have actualised this already. However, you only have to turn on the news to see that this is not the case. As people of colour, we must always choose a side and be deliberate in our stance. Indifference on issues that directly affect our communities will ensure that these problems persist.

9. Never change teams

"Don't trust people whose feelings change with time. Trust people whose feelings remain the same even when the time changes."
– Bob Marley

Description

As your social status changes and you find yourself moving in different circles, it can be difficult to continue to see things as you previously saw them. You could be in your newfound position through shear hard work, good fortune or the grace of others; however, the more time spent there produces a type of amnesia which can result in having contempt for people who look like you but are not at the same societal level. Try not to lose sight of who you actually are though.

The Flip-flopper

He had us bobbing our heads in the club to a song about Jesus. He made it okay to question why we're studying at university and taught us NOT to be mindless sheep. He took hip hop back to its core and hit us with bar after bar of rhythmic rhymes that were so carefully constructed, even the fussiest critic couldn't find fault with his talent. He came across as a poetic voice for a generation who could also do something wicked with an old-school tune that had your mama singing along too. He was a loose cannon who, on live TV, openly criticised the then president's response to aiding black people in a time of national crisis by boldly telling the world, "George Bush doesn't care about black people." We all felt that, and he said it for US. And yet in 2018, this same man was seen in a MAGA (Make America Great Again) hat explaining why he pledges allegiance to Donald Trump. This parable is not meant to attack mental health issues or make light of someone's inner turmoil. What it is meant to do is make you understand how it looks to others when one of US so publicly falls from a position amongst OUR people. It's a hard pill to swallow when a person seemingly understands OUR struggles, backs US up and then over time (and possibly a fatter bank account) forges a bridge to the other side and switches teams.

The New Neighbourhood

Moving into his dream house gave Dwayne a sense of accomplishment. He had worked hard for many years to get to the suburbs. Dwayne worked his way up to a managerial position at the warehouse and was finally earning good money, the kind of money which meant he could move his family out of the inner city and into the leafy green district where all the houses had picket fences. As Dwayne sat in his armchair hearing birds instead of police sirens, he was overcome with pride. At that moment, he heard the doorbell ring. His wife told Dwayne not to bother getting up as she was already on her way to opening the door.

He could hear the excitement in Charlotte's voice as she spoke to the people on the doorstep. Wondering who was there, Dwayne got up out of his chair and walked over to the door. To his surprise he saw a black couple standing there, the wife with a pie in her hands handing it over to Charlotte. They then exchanged a few pleasantries before his wife thanked them and closed the door. "What's up, you look like you saw a ghost?" asked Charlotte. "Yeah, the ghosts of ghettos past," replied Dwayne. Charlotte put the pie down on the side and folded her arms, "And what's that supposed to mean?" she asked in a stern voice. Dwayne rested himself on the arm of the couch, "I didn't move us all the way out here to have to see the same people who we were trying to get away from."

Summary

The phrase sour grapes came from Aesop's fable about a fox reaching for some grapes. Once he realised he couldn't get them, he turned around and walked off. Some crows who were observing the whole thing from nearby asked the fox why he left the grapes. The fox responded by telling the crows that the grapes were sour, so he didn't want them. Now in life, sometimes people will tell you they don't want something when it's exactly what they want more than anything in the world. They'll tell you they don't want it because they believe it's unattainable. Some people will beat the drum of their people whilst there in it and believe that there is no other option, but if they get an opportunity outside their community, they'll switch over faster than you can say *Judas*. Only problem is that once the other community no longer want them then they have nowhere to go. We have seen this play out so many times over the years, and sadly the person is usually all too happy to change sides. They proceed with this even though history has shown us that, often, those who switch over, are usually discarded once they have served their purpose.

10. Always celebrate our successes

"Work hard to discover your gift and you will never envy or hate another human being who is manifesting theirs."
– Louis Farrakhan

Description

Most of us have probably experienced the occasional feeling of jealously or envy, but we can agree that it is dreadful behaviour to exhibit. There are some people within our community who suffer with these ill feelings. More often than not, they seem to display them when discussing the success of their own people. They're the type of people who see someone who looks like them, who appears to have more than they do and instead of trying to learn from that person, they decide to hold bitterness toward them.

The Rapper

In 2020, the New York rapper Pop Smoke was murdered by masked men at a house he was renting in Beverly Hills. The media reported the crime as a robbery gone wrong, but there was no evidence to suggest that anything was taken from the property. Earlier that day, the rapper had posted on social media about a few gifts he had recently received. He also shared pictures of him sitting in an expensive car with his friends holding large amounts of cash. In both posts, a portion of the address was visible in the photos. In paying her last respects to the rapper, Nikki Minaj expressed what a lot of people were already thinking, "The Bible tells us that jealousy is as cruel as the grave," insinuating that it may have been done by someone who was resentful of his success.

The Man and His New Car

Summer 2010 in New York City was hot as hell and everyone had their windows up and AC on full blast. Well almost everyone. Isiah had his windows down as he wanted to be seen by as many people as possible. Isiah had just purchased a late model big body German coupe, with cream interior and Italian leather seats. Earlier that day, Isiah walked into a showroom on eleventh avenue with a backpack full of hundred dollar bills (which he withdrew from his bank an hour prior). Isiah was a property developer who had just made his first big cash windfall and decided to treat himself to the car that he had always wanted. He hadn't eaten all day and had his heart set on some fried chicken, the kind grandma made, so he parked up on Dr Martin Luther King Boulevard and stepped out of his new pride and joy.

There were some guys sitting on a wall across the street who were a similar age to Isiah, so he looked across and gave a nod of acknowledgement to show respect. Surprisingly, the guys ignored his gesture, but Isiah was too pumped up to be bothered and went on into the shop to place his order. As Isiah was looking through the menu, one of the guys who was sitting on the wall walked in and began looking at the board too. He was complaining about the price rises and was trying to haggle with the owner, but the restaurateur was not budging, "The price is the price," he said, firmly. Isiah was in good spirits, so he offered to pay for the man's meal. The man looked at Isiah in disbelief, "Why would you do that for me?" Isiah just responded by saying, "The last few months have been good to me and I always try to help a brother out whenever I can." The man went on to tell Isiah, "I've fallen on hard times and can't seem to catch a break." They continued talking whilst they waited for their food. It turned out that the man was a painter and decorator, so Isiah told him how he needed someone in that field, and he had work for him. Their food arrived and Isiah asked the man to follow him to his car so he could give him his business card. As Isiah got to his car, he noticed a huge deep key scratch on the hood of his new vehicle. Isiah was horrified. "Who the hell would do this?" he asked as he held his head in his hand. The man looked over at Isiah and said, "I'm so sorry, I had no idea. I figured you'd be a jerk."

The Hammer

In 1991, Stanley Burrell, better known by his stage name M.C. Hammer, was at the height of his fame with the release of his popular album in 1990, *Please Hammer Don't Hurt 'Em*. It went on to become the first hip-hop record to be certified diamond. What made this achievement so impressive was that M.C. Hammer did it the hard way and in a relatively short space of time. Only a few years earlier, M.C. Hammer was selling his records from the trunk of his car. He independently released his first album and promoted it himself by performing live in clubs around the Bay area of California. This gained the attention of Capitol Records, who were keen to sign him. When it came time to negotiate a contract, Hammer was in a position to dictate his own terms.

Once signed on with Capitol, Hammer employed over two hundred people with the vast majority being friends who he had grown up with. He definitely had the mentality of leaving nobody behind even though it was costing him a staggering amount each month in wages. Despite all this, his success was not celebrated by his fellow rappers; in fact, he was ridiculed and mocked by many of his peers. The reason they gave for their constant pokes at Hammer was that he was a sell-out or just not street enough. Hammer never claimed to be anything other than what he was, which was an entertainer. Los Angeles rapper Ice-T confirmed what many already believed in a verse from his 1991 album O.G. Original Gangster where he said, "A special shout out is going out to the one and only MC Hammer; A lot of people diss you man, they just jealous..."

Summary

Don't you go on to do even better and achieve even greater things when you've got cheerleaders in your corner, sharing in the jubilations of your victories? Remember when you were a kid and you did well at something — maybe you aced a test, won first place or even just beat your big bro in a video game? How much better did you feel about your triumph when someone else rejoiced along with you? In a world with more than enough quick-fingered keyboard warriors waiting to hate on other folks' successes, we need to be voices of positivity for each other. We not only need to cheer for one another, but we need to show up and show out in large numbers. Solidarity is key in both promoting individual success and strengthening our communities. Our children need to see us backing each other so that they in turn will back their fellow brothers and sisters.

11. Never speak negatively of black people in front of non-black people

"An envious heart makes a treacherous ear."
– Zora Neale Hurston

Description

When we speak on black issues, depending on our audience, we can appear like a spokesperson for all black people. With that in mind, we should be careful not to discuss internal matters candidly with other people. Sometimes things are said in haste and can be taken out of context as the internal politics may well be lost on that group. In other words, what siblings might say about their parents in private would be very different to what they would say about them publicly.

The Fever

In a seemingly candid conversation between two co-workers, Chris explained his love for Caucasian women to his white colleague, particularly blonde ones, by saying that they are easier to deal with and less work than girls he grew up with. He said things like, "Black girls are just so high maintenance and expect you to pretty much jump through hoops to gain their affection. But then these same *sistas* get all angry when they see me with a white girl. Go figure." Though the conversation seemed innocuous, one thing that appeared clear was that Chris made a distinction between these Caucasian women and black women.

Now don't misunderstand me, there is nothing wrong with finding beauty and even love with a person outside of your race. But...must you do so at the expense of your own people? When one publicly states that the women of their own race are angry, hard work or less attractive, the rest of the world hears the message loud and clear. Instead of being seen as a love for another race, it typically comes off as some sort of self-hatred and contempt for your own.

The Timekeeper

Being on time was something that Percy prided himself on, making lateness his ultimate pet peeve. While he was working late one evening, he decided to order food for him and his colleague. Ian convinced Percy to order some Caribbean food as he loved hot and spicy cuisine. Percy was reluctant to make the call and kept making other suggestions, but Ian kept pushing for him to place the order, "Percy, come on, call it through, my mouth is watering for some jerk chicken. You've got West Indian roots, so I know you'll enjoy it even more than me." Percy finally called the order through and was given a thirty-minute waiting time.

He set a twenty-nine-minute countdown on his phone. They both continued with work as they waited for their meals to arrive. Percy was then startled by the phone alarm indicating that the countdown had ended, "You see, this is why I didn't want to order Caribbean because black people are always late. They can never be on time for anything. I've never used that place before, but I knew they would operate on black people time. Typical, so typical." Before he got a chance to finish his rant the buzzer rang, and Ian went down to collect the food. The following week Ian was chairing a project meeting that was for a nine o'clock start. Percy's morning train was delayed which meant that he arrived at the meeting ten minutes late. As he walked in, he apologised for arriving late and proceeded to give the reason why. One of the people in the meeting stopped him and answered, "It's ok Percy, Ian already explained that you were just operating on black people's time." The whole room burst out laughing to which Percy could only look over at Ian and give an awkward smile.

Summary

We have enough people speaking against us without us doing it too; therefore, we should do our best to counteract any negative speech with positive words. And, please, black men and women, if you must have these conversations at all (because sometimes we need to vent), do not do so in a public forum or amongst mixed company where your words might be misconstrued and potentially later used against us, all of us. Everyone is listening to you as the representative. Don't screw it up.

12. Choose the right partner

"The mate you choose will either inspire you to grow into your greatness or confine you to complacency. They'll either be your other half or make you half of yourself."
– Nuri Muhammad

Description

In many cultures, the right to choose is removed when selecting a partner. One of the reasons given is that a mother can choose a better wife for her son than if the son was left to choose for himself. The same goes for the father picking a husband for his daughter. The parent will call upon their experience, expertise and other deciding factors when making the decision, factors which a younger person would not necessarily take into consideration. However, in western culture, guys and girls generally just pick partners based on very rudimentary characteristics, usually very much in the moment. We would all have heard the old adage *opposites attract*; if we're talking about magnets, then yes that is undoubtedly correct because the opposite poles of each magnet are indeed drawn to each other. Yet if given the choice, a human being will choose to surround themselves with like-minded people. For example, rich people do not seek the company of poor people. It is the poor who want to be part of the wealthy inner circle. The same principle can be applied across other groups: those who perceive themselves to be ugly will be attracted to those who they believe to be beautiful, but not the other way around – just like the weak are attracted to the strong, or the unpopular are attracted to the popular. This can sometimes fool people into thinking that opposites do attract, but like a magnet, other metals are just naturally attracted to it.

The Chocolate-Vanilla Swirl

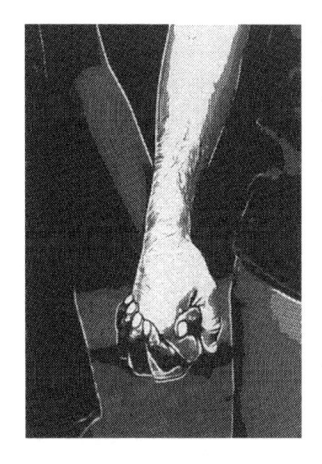

Naomi was always a very liberal girl. She grew up in a cosmopolitan city and had friends from all different backgrounds, so dating outside of her race was not a taboo. Even though race was never a factor when choosing a partner, it wasn't until she was in her late twenties that she dated outside her race. She met Jake through work. He was a handsome, charming thirtysomething who managed the finance department. Although this was Naomi's first experience of an interracial relationship, Jake was somewhat of the expert having only ever dated black women. When Naomi asked the question, what is it that he liked about black women, Jake rattled off a response like he had said it a thousand times before. He spoke of his love for darker complexions and the beauty of the skin tones. Naomi was flattered and didn't give too much thought to his response to her question.

Starting off strong, the two were dating for several months and they had many of the same interests. Connecting them was their taste in music, food, holiday destinations and they liked the same types of TV shows. It was an easy relationship for them both to be in; everything just worked. They didn't have any disagreements until one day that all changed. Naomi was around Jake's house sitting on the couch channel-hopping, while Jake was in the kitchen making dinner. Naomi started watching the news where they were reporting the death of Eric Garner. This was the first time she was hearing about it. She was understandably horrified as she watched the footage of an unarmed man being choked to death by a group of police officers on a New York street.

Eric's crime was allegedly selling cigarettes illegally on a street corner. Naomi called Jake from the kitchen to look at what she was seeing. Jake rushed from the kitchen wondering what all the fuss was about. Naomi began explaining what she had just saw. Though he thought the killing was a bit brutal, Jake shrugged his shoulders and responded by saying that he shouldn't have been selling cigarettes. His nonchalant response offended Naomi, so much that she immediately left and went back to her apartment that evening. Naomi avoided Jake for a few days until Jake managed to catch up with her at work. He apologised for what appeared to be a lack of empathy toward the situation and said he would make it up to her by taking her out for a meal and then they could watch a movie back at his place. Jake did have a way with words and Naomi accepted his apology and agreed to the date night. They went out to an Indian restaurant and when they got back to Jake's place, he took out the newly released DVD of 12 Years a Slave for them to watch. Naomi was excited as she heard about the film due to its success at that year's Academy awards. The film proved to be very heart-wrenching and as the final credits rolled down the screen, Naomi was still in tears and visibly shaken. Jake thinking on how best to get Naomi out of her sad state puts his foot in it again by telling her that she shouldn't be upset because it was such a long time ago.

The Three-Piece Suit

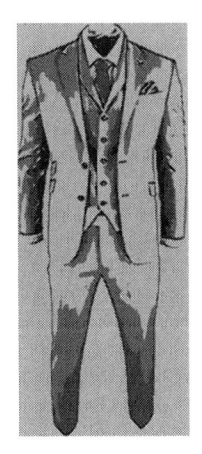

Trevor, affectionately known as Three-piece because he would always be immaculately dressed in a fine suit, was a very serious man. Hardened by the racism he faced growing up in a small town in 1960s England, he was very outspoken against racial injustice. He would call it out whenever he saw it raise its ugly head. Three-piece knew he wanted to make a difference from very early on in his life and studied meticulously throughout his youth and eventually had his own law firm. Three-piece wasn't interested in making millions, that's not why he got into law. He wanted to give something back, something that he never got when he was coming up. That was a role model and someone who cared about the community. The bulk of Three-piece's work was racial discrimination cases: he fought for the underdog and on many occasions won. He was very good at what he did.

Three-piece seemed to be obsessed with race. He would always be angry about what he saw as inequalities in society. A day wouldn't go past without him discussing some topic about race. Although his wife had the patience of a saint, even she could be heard groaning the words, "Here we go again," every now and then. You see Three-piece's wife was a white lady; they had been married for ten years at this point and had three beautiful children. His wife Wendy was a lovely woman and they had met when he was in his final year of university. Naturally, she loved his passion for political injustice. She too saw herself as an activist and fought for social change. You might be surprised to hear that Three-piece was married to a woman of European descent, but you have to think of the psychology behind his decision. Three-piece suffered at lot of racial abuse throughout his childhood which caused him to grow into a very angry man. He knew before he even had kids that he didn't want his children to have to go through what he went through. On a subconscious level, Three-piece believed that by having a white wife he would encounter less discrimination and his offspring would have it easier than he did. Although on a conscious level, he was still very bitter and would be described as having a chip on his shoulder.

Three-piece just didn't know how to turn it off – he could be watching TV and then refuse to finish the show because he would see something that he thought was racist. Wendy tried very hard to encourage Three-piece to ease up a little as the years passed, but it didn't work. He seemed to get angrier and more cantankerous the older he got as Wendy thought that he would often see racism where it didn't actually exist. Three-piece's discontent pushed Wendy away, even when she did her best to try to sympathise with his plight.

Their children grew, and sadly none of them followed in his footsteps by going into the profession of law. His eldest son became a paramedic, the second went into accountancy, and his daughter became an interior designer. They also had no interest in being revolutionaries or fighting against social injustice. However, they all followed his example by choosing white partners to marry.

The Clubber

When he first saw Cassandra in the club that night, he knew from that moment he had to make her his girl. Earl could charm the birds from the trees and wasted no time in talking to Cassandra. He was a master persuader and didn't take long to have Cassandra hanging onto his every word. As the night ended, they exchanged contact details and agreed to meet up sometime soon.

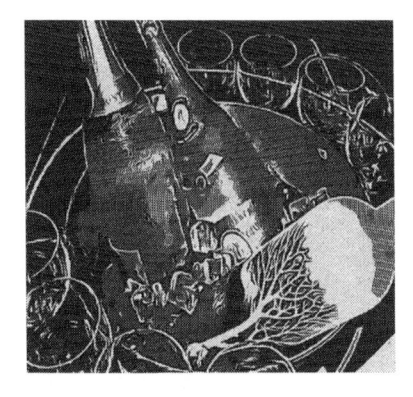

Earl spared no expense and took Cassandra on date after date, each one being more impressive than the previous. Although Cassandra was an extremely beautiful lady, Earl was introducing her to things that she had never experienced before. After a few weeks, the two became an item, Earl loved showing her off to his friends in person and to his enemies through social media. He would put posts up of the two of them in his top of the range 4x4 vehicle or on nights out often with the caption *livin' my best life* underneath the photo. They eventually moved in together and started taking exotic holidays to far out destinations, which of course were all captured for his social media.

After a couple of years Earl found that he wanted more from the relationship. Now in his early thirties, he started seeing the world differently. Cassandra hadn't reached thirty yet, and she still very much enjoyed the bars, clubs and the standard beach holiday twice a year. The more time they spent together, the more Earl noticed just how few things that they had in common. He was so mesmerised by her beauty that he never took the time to listen to Cassandra's interests, beliefs or core values for that matter. He was too focused on the goal of making her his woman and didn't care to have any conversations of depth. It was then that he realised how much he had changed since then. He'd matured, no longer into the things he was into previously in his youth. Earl was more politically aware and socially conscious. Cutting a rug on a nightclub dance floor was far from his mind. Moving to the next stage of his life was primarily on his agenda, so he sat down to have a conversation with Cassandra. He started with, "I feel that we have become different people, and I would like us to see how we can move the relationship forward." Cassandra put her phone down before answering, "The only different person is you. I've stayed the same, you've turned into an old man."

Summary

Whom you choose to partner up with in this life may singularly be the most important decision you ever make. You may think it's your career or where you decide to live or if you choose to become a vegetarian or just enjoy that cheeseburger. But the truth is, all those decisions are dependent on whom you spend your life with. When done correctly, picking a partner means picking a life companion who will aid you in making your biggest moves and who will spend, by far, the most time with you. You may have made all the decisions above prior to meeting that special someone and then they come along and undo every single one because we tend to adapt to the ones closest to us. Therefore, that person needs to be in complete agreement with what your goals and ambitions are. This partner must push you forward, never hold you back (and vice versa of course).

Surely anyone can help you to be the best version of yourself. After all, love knows no race nor colour and can literally be found anywhere. This is absolutely true. Real love in and of itself is colour-blind. Provided that your lover has the same productive and positive mind-set as this also means that you two can make each other the whole version of yourselves. However, part of your whole self is your blackness. This is a part of you that you are embracing, loving and sharing with the rest of the world. Yet, in this scenario, the one where you pick a non-black counterpart, you are kind of showing the rest of us that this is your preference, even though you may have simply chosen this person based on all your other connections (placing no emphasis on their lack of melanin). Nonetheless, you may have children who go on to choose non-black partners, simply following your example. Their children may then take non-black partners too, and so on and so forth. This may continue so that after a few generations, no one of your lineage even knows they ever had a drop of Africa coursing through their veins at all. Is that a problem? Well, maybe not for some. But for those who are proud of their blackness and rate all that accompanies it, it may be a bit disappointing to learn that your great grandchildren may not even recognise that they are black at all.

13. Be an ambassador at all times

"Each person must live their life
as a model for others."
– Rosa Parks

Description

The term role model is something usually reserved for athletes or celebrities in the entertainment business because they typically have a young impressionable following. With this position, they should have a responsibility to set a good example. An ambassador, however, is sent by a state as its permanent representative in a foreign country. As the diaspora, we are often in a country where we are the minority. So, by default, we become an unknowing and usually unwilling ambassador of our race.

The Ladies' Man

Mikey was a young dynamic man who had not long graduated from an Ivy League school with a bachelor's degree in social science. Mikey moved to New York searching for those big bucks from one of those Fortune 500 companies. His area of expertise was business analysis and it wasn't too long before he got his first interview. It wasn't the large company he had hoped for, but Mikey was hyped up and did his due diligence prior to the interview by researching the company. There was a three-stage process: a telephone interview; if he was successful, there would be a meeting with the team leader; and lastly, a one to one with the CEO, Larry Tovak. Mikey blew past the telephone interview and impressed the team leader during the face-to-face interview. Now he just waited for a call to confirm a time for the final stage. He was confident as the lady who interviewed him previously indicated that he was the standout candidate. Confirmation came through as he had expected, and he arrived in good time for his interview with Larry Tovak.

The interview followed the structure just as Mikey had anticipated. The pair spoke about his credentials and his ability to do the job. Once all the serious stuff was out of the way he then asked Mikey what his interests and hobbies were outside of work. Mikey gave the standard response of how he liked to watch and play sports. The CEO then went on to ask Mikey if he was a ladies' man. Mikey not giving too much thought to the question just replied with a, "Yeah, I guess so." The meeting wrapped up shortly after and Mikey felt positive about how the interview went. In fact, he was totally surprised when he heard back from the company informing him that he was unsuccessful. Mikey didn't dwell on that too long and very quickly found employment working for a Fortune 500 company as he originally set out to do. Unbeknownst to Mikey, only a year earlier there was a brother who worked for that company in sales. His name was Shawn and he had an eye for the ladies and the ladies had eyes for him too. He had a problem separating business from pleasure and it would often overlap. He ended up having a brief fling with Mrs Tovak, the wife of the CEO, which consequently resulted in him losing his job. The thing was that Mr Tovak didn't know many black men before Shawn and didn't know many after. In fact, Shawn was the first black guy who he spent a lot of time with, so everything that Shawn said and every action that Shawn took was a seen by Mr Tovak as a reflection of Shawn's entire race. Shawn was good at his job, which was a positive, but Shawn was reckless and unprofessional, which was a negative. When Mr Tovak interviewed Mikey, he accepted that he would be able to perform the role to a high standard because Shawn had already demonstrated that, albeit in a totally different role. However, Mr Tovak needed reassurance that Mikey could behave himself with the women in the office. Mikey, sadly, did not assuage his fears in that interview.

The Office Politics

Keisha was working in a call centre with a bunch of other young adults. Some were working their way through college, some working their way up through management and others just passing the time. She got along with her colleagues and often socialised outside of work for birthday get-togethers, mimosa brunches and even the random night out.

Once, they were all discussing what was happening around the Black Lives Matter Movement. They pretty much unanimously agreed that racism was a part of history but not the present. When Ted, who sat across from Keisha, asked her thoughts on it all, she coyly said, "I don't get into that kind of stuff."

He pushed her further to say, "But we've had a black president. Surely that's proof enough that we're post-racial now." Keisha was still firm in her position and said, "Eh, I just don't get into politics." Everybody loved Keisha because she was a down-to-earth girl who worked hard on the job, but she also never ruffled any feathers nor turned down a good time.

Amy was Keisha's work BFF, gossiping about all the others in the office, sharing stories, dating advice and naturally syncing their periods. Amy felt comfortable saying pretty much anything to Keisha. For example, when Keisha bedazzled her acrylic nails with tiny little jewels, Amy marvelled at how *ghetto- fabulous* they were. When Keisha opted for her natural short fro instead of her usual long braids, Amy couldn't help but pet her work BFF's hair saying how *soft* and *fluffy* it was. When they went to the beach, Amy naturally put her arm next to Keisha's and stated, "Look, I'm as dark as you." Even when they go to the club, Amy happily sings along to all the music, not missing a single chance to shout out *nigga* in every rap verse that allows it. In fact, when they went out for Ted's birthday, Amy was *nigga*-ing it up to the latest hip-hop tune when Eddie, the new brother in the office, stared at her in disbelief. She didn't know what his problem was and asked defiantly, "What?!" Eddie, stunned, said, "You can't say that." Amy was quick to reply, "Don't be ridiculous. I sing this with Keisha all the time. It's cool."

Summary

Some people will encounter just a handful of black people that they feel comfortable enough to interact with on a deeper level. You may be one of those black people. Nobody is saying you need to perpetually be donning a black power fist on your lapel, reciting Malcolm X lines whilst preaching about pan Africanism. But it would be nice if you could let people know what's up when they say or do something that you know your grandma would deem inappropriate. Some of you will moan, "But it's not my place to educate the ignorant. I don't care if they use the n word. So what if they want to touch my hair; they're just curious. Why is it our jobs to teach them? What a burden!" Consider this: When Europeans conquered our lands, did they grant us the same indifference? Nope. They considered it their mission to *teach* us. Whether we needed to *learn* their ways is definitely up for debate, but one thing that is certain is that when you leave your house, you represent us whether you like it or not. You might as well embrace it or at the very least, use it to your advantage and represent us right.

14. Never make excuses for racist behaviour

"In a racist society it is not enough to be non-racist, we must be anti-racist."
— *Angela Y. Davis*

Description

Every now and again we hear about a blatant act of racism that makes news across the world and people of all colours are outraged. The standard response is to condemn what the perpetrator said or did, and usually the offender will issue a public apology to pacify our community as they try to minimise the damage to their reputation or brand. All too often what we find is that one person from our community will defend the act which everybody else universally condemns. He will make all types of excuses and justifications on the person or organisations behalf.

The Actor

Actor Liam Neeson, famous for his roles in such films as Schindler's list, Star Wars and the Taken movies, made the headlines in 2019 for some inflammatory remarks. He was being interviewed about his upcoming film and spoke candidly about an incident over thirty years prior where a female friend told him about how she was raped. His friend explained to him that rather than reporting the crime to the police, she decided to just deal with it in her own way, but not before telling Liam Neeson that the assailant was a black man. Mr Neeson made no qualms telling the interviewer how he went out each night for several weeks looking to kill any random man of African descent.

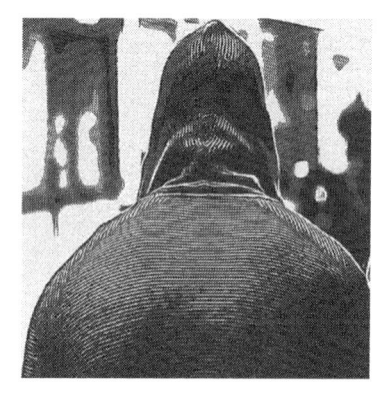

He was armed with a blunt object hoping to smash open a black skull. Now in Liam Neeson's defence, he did say that in retrospect he was ashamed that he behaved like that and he was now a changed man; however, people were obviously shocked to hear this testimony from the Hollywood star. Within the entertainment industry, people acted fast in condemning his foolish words.

Then enter John Barnes, former England international soccer player who appeared on Good Morning Britain claiming that Liam Neeson deserved a medal for what he said. Yes, you heard right. So, you have most white people in full agreement that Liam Neeson was completely out of order for his psychopathic admission, but then there's that one black guy who somehow manages to try and make sense out of the racism. John Barnes justified his *medal* statement by saying that he should be commended for his honesty. Now how on earth can someone, let alone a black person, say that a man who admits that he walked the streets looking to kill a random black man needs to be commended? Would he still say that Liam Neeson deserved a medal if it was him whom he ran into on one of those nights?

The Groundskeeper

Kevon and his son David would often get into arguments. The frequency increased the older his son got. David was now in his final year of high school and was at that stage when you realise your parents are fallible. Kevon saw the world very differently to how many others saw it. You could even make a case that Kevon suffered with cognitive bias, the inability to be subjective on certain topics which can lead to being judgemental due to improperly assessing individual situations. This would become apparent whenever race came up. Kevon grew up in the south but moved with his wife to West Philadelphia when he was in his thirties. David was born a few years later, then followed by a couple more children. Kevon was a hardworking man, always complied with the rules and wanted the best for his kids. He worked as a groundskeeper for a very wealthy family for over twenty years. He was paid well, had a good healthcare package, and was treated like part of the family. However, Kevon lived in West Philly, and although most of the people in the area were like him in the sense that they were law-abiding and hardworking citizens, there were a few bad apples.

These rotten fruits, who were often up to no good, would get into trouble with the police, making them the cause for most of the crime in the neighbourhood. All the criminals who Kevon saw were African-American due to him living in an overwhelmingly black area. The only white people who Kevon knew personally was the family he worked for, a very wealthy, liberal-minded group of individuals. Over time, this warped Kevon's reality. In turn, many conflicts ensued between Kevon and his son.

When David would bring his friends around to the house, Kevon would make assumptions that his friends were *delinquents* purely based on how they were dressed; Kevon was just so out of touch. David would tell his father stories of being stopped by the police for no reason – this happened on several occasions. Kevon would respond by telling David that if he dressed like a thug, then he should expect to be treated like a thug.

One day, Kevon was asked by his employers if he could take their teenage daughter across town to her dance class, something he had done previously. Katherine, the daughter, saw Kevon as an uncle because she had known him her whole life. On this occasion, Kevon was stopped by the police. They told him that there had been a report of a young girl fitting Katherine's description who had been spotted in an older African-American male's vehicle showing signs of distress. They asked Kevon to step out of the car and as he proceeded to follow their instructions, the officer grabbed him and threw his head down on top of the car hood. The hood was hot, so Kevon jumped back due to the heat. As he did that, the other officer rushed over and began handcuffing him. The two officers were restraining him on the floor. Once he was fully restrained, one of the officers questioned him while the other was talking to Katherine. After about five minutes, the officer came back and said that the girl's story matched up with his. They then let them go on their way.

When the two of them arrived back to the family house, Katherine told her parents of the shocking ordeal. Stan, the father, was understandably outraged and wanted to submit a complaint to the police department. Kevon was originally trying to deter them from pursuing anything as he said that it was a case of mistaken identity. Stan pointed to the cut marks and bruises on Kevon's face and neck area. He told him that regardless of the situation, they shouldn't have handled him that way. Kevon started to think that maybe Stan did have a point and that the police had used rough house tactics due to racial profiling. "Ok Stan, I think we should put a complaint in," said Kevon. Stan took out a notepad and pen. "Talk me through what happened when the police came to the car door," said Stan. Kevon replied, "The officer asked me to get out of the car, so I reached for my licence and then he just grabbed me by my neck and threw me on top of the hood." Stan stopped him, "Wait, hold on. So, he saw you reach for something? He must have thought you had a gun." Kevon nodded his head in agreement "Of course, I forgot I did that. Yeah, because up until that point they were being normal. It was my own fault."

Summary

It may feel harmless to defend your fellow man in their seemingly innocuous transgressions. You may even feel compelled to explain away their behaviour, a bit like how Donald Trump's camp would often try to make sense of his tweets by saying things like, "What he meant to say was this…" Although you may just want to make peace with everyone to help the world be a better and more loving place, you're doing more damage than good. Racist behaviour is never okay. Racist thoughts and actions need to be recognised for exactly what they are so that the rest of us can decide whether this is a teachable moment, or we should just completely steer clear of the racist perpetrator. Teachable moments are for those who say kinda racist things but do so because they know no better. Said persons could potentially be converted if a loving black person, like yourself, shows them the light. These are your co-workers who just want to touch your hair because they're curious; those *Karens* need to be educated, not necessarily chastised and whipped. Yet even in their re-education, you are still NOT to excuse their behaviour. On the other hand, you have the self-proclaimed racists who make flippant comments and exhibit blatantly racist behaviour because that's just how they feel and will continue to feel 'til they no longer feel breath. Expose those folks. Vilify them. Let everyone know their intentions and then counter them by demonstrating how great we actually are.

15. Discontinue the use of colonial belief systems

"I freed a thousand slaves; I could have freed a thousand more if only they knew they were slaves."
– Harriet Tubman

Description

Slavery may have ended in the late 1800s for the African diaspora across North America, South America and the Caribbean, yet colonial belief systems remain just as strong as they did two hundred years ago for many of our people. You could ask the average African-American, Afro-Brazilian, Dominican or Haitian a certain set of question on race and you would get a universal response even though they have varied cultures and speak four different languages. This is a result of hundreds of years of brainwashing which continues to get passed down from generation to generation.

The Master Plan

William was a British slave owner in the West Indies. He was invited to the colony of Virginia in the early 1700s to educate the slave owners of that region on his successful techniques of control. A large crowd gathered to hear William speak as many of the owners in the area had troublesome field hands, and he boasted to have never had an issue with a single soul on his plantation. This was a bold statement: everybody had the odd runaway or unruly one in their possession, but William said that he didn't experience these rebels. All the wild claims now had to be backed up as he took to the stage to proceed in delivering his presentation. The crowd stood unwearyingly in anticipation, much of the crowd praying for him to be the real deal, next to them were the haters who were hoping to expose him as a charlatan.

As he started speaking it became apparent very quickly that he was the truth. He had a system that had not been heard by the ears of these simple people of Virginia before. You could see the crowd silently looking at each other in amazement with their mouths gaped open as he continued with his speech. William mentioned that he took differences amongst the slave population and then made them bigger. For example, he said that he used skin tones and played the darker skinned folk against the lighter skinned ones. He pit old against young, male versus female. He spoke of the importance to create distrust amongst the slaves but ensure complicit trust toward the slave owner. William went into great depths on the psychology behind his methods. He finally closed by assuring the audience that if his system was implemented correctly then the parents will teach their children this ideology for generations. As you can imagine, the crowd rushed back as fast as they could to hurry and put their newfound knowledge into immediate practice.

The N Word

From as long as Chris could remember, he always knew of the word. He heard it so much growing up that he genuinely thought it was like a term of endearment, similar to baby or love. Unless you did something wrong of course, then it sounded very different. The word was versatile like that. It wasn't just in his house that he heard it either. By the time he started school, the older kids would call each other it. And once he developed a taste in music, all the artists that he listened to were saying it on all their tracks. The word was just something that was always there, and Chris never gave it any thought. Chris also never heard anyone other than black people use the word.

However, there was one house which Chris would go to where he never heard the word said – that was at his friend Malik's place. Malik's parents didn't talk the same way that Chris would hear his parents speak. They would refer to him as young man or little king, and Chris never heard them use any cuss words, ever. When Chris was sixteen and trying to figure things out, he was curious as to why he never heard them use the n word, so one Saturday afternoon when he was hanging out around their house he just came out and asked the question. Mr Brown didn't answer the question directly, he just walked over to their bookshelf and handed Chris two books. "If you want to know the reason then read these," Malik's dad said. Mr Brown was a very serious man, so Chris did just as he was told and replied, "Yes sir, I'll read them." Chris wasn't too big on reading but knew that he had to finish the books before he could go back round to Malik's because Mr Brown would ask him if he had read them. Chris started reading the first book, which although it was, heavy reading, it had Chris gripped. He blew through the first and couldn't wait to get stuck into the second one. He found that book every bit as enjoyable as the first one.

A week had passed, and Chris went back over to Malik's house to return the books to Mr Brown. "What did you think?" asked Mr Brown. Chris replied, "I think I understand now why you don't use that word, sir." Mr Brown's face was still serious as he replied, "I haven't uttered that word in thirty years, but it's not about me. I already read those books a long time ago. What about you, what are you going to do?" Malik came into the room at that time too and he stopped what he was doing to hear the response to his dad's question. Chris then cleared his throat and made his declaration, "I had no idea what that word even meant, but knowing what I now know, I can't use that word again." Mr Brown's face lit up with pride and even his stern face made a half smile.

Later that day, Chris went back home and as he walked through the backdoor. His dad was sitting there eating ribs. "Ya'll want some of dis?" asked his father whilst trying to watch the football game. Chris decided to share what he had learned earlier with Malik's dad, "Dad, I've been doing some research into the n word and I've made a decision not to say it anymore as we degrade ourselves by using it." Chris's father was sucking on the bone and replied as he was taking a sip of his cherry cola, "N**** pleeeeasse."

The Brazilian Grandmother

As Avo Santos held her granddaughter for the very first time, she was overwhelmed with a sense of pride. This was a normal feeling to exhibit when you see your grandchild, but for Avo Santos she felt a sense of completion. It was a similar sensation to what a marathon runner experiences when they finally cross the finish line. Avo Santos kept comparing her shiny black skin to that of the new-born baby's pearly white complexion. The baby's hair already had curls, but Avo didn't seem to mind too much because the hair was golden blonde. Her prayers were answered when the baby opened her eyes to reveal their bright blue hue. Avo Santos thanked the Lord for blessing her with such a beautiful grandchild. This was because Avo was from a generation that viewed blackness as a stain that needed to be removed. Her mother discouraged her from bringing a boy home who was darker than her. Avo went above and beyond her mother's advice and married white in order to guarantee the next generation to be lighter. She then encouraged her daughters to do the same as she did so that they could continue to improve the bloodline.

Summary

The n word may seem like a harmless term, a word that's even been described as taking the negative and oppressive term *nigger* and reappointing it for our own purposes. The thing is, it's not. We may use it affectionately amongst our brothers, but we are also quick to call a good-for-nothing brother an n word too. In fact, we use it interchangeably to refer to any brother, sometimes using it to even refer to a non-black person. We sprinkle it in a lot of our underground and mainstream music alike, allowing nonpersons of colour to sing along freely. And then, we get offended when they do? But why? Because we own the rights to it? Answer me this, what other ethnic group or people have adopted a pejorative that was once used against them in various dehumanising techniques and now use it affectionately? A word that becomes the last thing a young brother may hear the moment before being killed in some senseless neighbourhood shooting. We need to stop seeing the world through a Eurocentric lens.

16. Love your hair

"I feel that the kinks, curls, or tight coils in Afro hair is beautiful and unique. No other race on this planet has hair like ours - that makes me proud."
– Monica Millner

Description

You may have heard this before, but I'll put it in here for those who need a gentle reminder: YOUR HAIR IS YOUR CROWN; WEAR IT WITH PRIDE. For decades, marketing executives mocked our need to conform to European hair aesthetics by selling us lotions and potions which we shellacked onto our hair like science experiments (remember the jheri curl). We have consumed everything from magic straightening creams to actually sewing another person's hair onto our own.

Ironically, Europeans throughout history have imitated the fullness of our locks, along with our curl patterns and intricately braided styles.

The Baby with the *Good* Hair

Many little white babies are often born bald. Their hair doesn't seem to come into its own until they're at least mobile. On the other hand, little black babies will often come pre-stocked with a lustrous shiny little crown of curls that grows so beautifully that mamas refuse to cut their baby boy's locks for some time because the hair is just too pretty. While black people have all different hair types and textures that grow at different rates and display in various shapes as they peek out of the roots of our scalps, a discussion tends to take place when the baby's hair starts to *form*.

Picture this — a mother enters the playground with her new baby, about 8 months old, and her older child, about 4 years old. The older child has tighter, kinkier curls that form into a stunning afro. The kind of hair that doesn't necessarily seem long by European standards, but when stretched out of its dormant shrinkage, one can see its impressive length. The baby, on the other hand, appears to have very loose curls, some don't even stand up just yet, sitting flat on her little head. The mother walks up to a group of mothers who haven't seen the newest member of the family since she was born and what's the first thing they say when feasting their eyes on that adorable little puddin'? I'm sure you can hear it, "Look at at her hair, so pretty. She's going to have good hair; you can tell from now." The mother probably responds with something like, "Yeah, girl. My oldest girl's hair was already *nappier* at this age. I think this baby will have much nicer hair than hers and mine. She probably takes after her, blah blah blah." At this point, who has tuned into this foolishness? Is the other child within earshot? What about the other beautiful babies with kinky coils who sit for hours to get their crown immaculately braided? If they don't have this baby's *good* hair, do they have *bad* hair?

It comes as no surprise that black girls with the kinkiest of curls have been playfully wrapping a towel around their head pretending to have that *Rapunzel, Rapunzel, let down your hair* length since Plymouth Rock. Whipping that towel back and forth, immersed in imaginative play, those girls are acting out having *good*, long, flowing European hair that doesn't grow from their own heads. But they wish it did. From the earliest of ages, many of us set our offspring up to believe that the hair they have is somehow inferior to a white person's hair or another black person with a looser curl pattern to their own.

The Little Black Girl

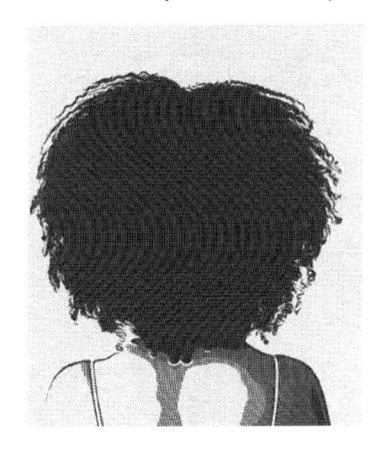

Little Layla was a precocious five-year-old. Born to a fair-skinned mother of British descent and Jamaican father, she was well versed in both the queen's English and patois with a sophisticated enough palate to handle a Sunday roast beef dinner and some scotch bonnet spiced BBQ jerk chicken wings for supper. Layla had a head full of beautifully wiry, tight curls. As her hair grew longer, her mother struggled to maintain it. She would tell the girl's father that it was just too knotty. The family had moved to the Midlands for the father's job so neither of them had any family close by. Occasionally, his family would visit, and they would braid Layla's hair. But the visits weren't frequent enough for the mother who had to cope with this unfamiliar texture of hair on a daily basis. She resigned to the fact that she would never learn to style it as well as the relatives could, and it would cost too much to get it done at the salon every couple of weeks. She just brushed it into a high little poof on the top of Layla's cute little head. But the dad wasn't satisfied with the same style day in and day out. He told the mother that she needed to sort it out and find someone who could manage their daughter's hair.

Eventually, the mother took the girl to an afro hair salon in the town centre and asked for their advice. The hairdresser said that the best thing to do was to relax it straight. By this time, little Layla was almost eight years old and was quite excited at the prospect of having hair just like mummy's. They booked an appointment for the following week, the longest week of Layla's life. When she arrived at the salon, she leapt into the chair and had a million questions for the stylist. The hairdresser applied the perm cream to her hair, section by section. She told her that it had to sit on her head for a bit and to let her know if it felt like it was burning. Layla sat patiently, waiting for something to happen. It took a while, but finally she felt the burning sensation she was warned about.

The hairdresser promptly washed it out and continued to style her hair. When she finished, Layla could not believe her eyes. She couldn't stop staring at herself in the mirror. She flipped her hair back and forth so many times, she almost got whiplash. Her mother came to collect her from the salon, and she ran to her, screaming, "Mummy, mummy, look at my hair. It's just so silky and long. It's, it's…It's a like a white girl's hair!"

Summary

We inadvertently inflict this form of self-hatred on each other even though Europeans have always admired every curl structure ever to grace our gorgeous black bodies. You know this, right? In the twentieth century, we can see that famous folks of European descent renamed our braided styles and passed them off as their own. They invented curly perms to achieve our volume. This has continued in the twenty-first century with many white women living vicariously through the curls of their black babies of dual heritage. If you look further back in history, you can see when full wigs became a staple of King Charles' high society in seventeenth century England. Wealthy Europeans of the colonial era seemed to never leave home without their wigs. Yet those wigs, although typically white, resembled the frizz and fullness of African hair. Some will say they were trying to adorn their heads with hair they couldn't grow, much like our babies with the long Rapunzel towels. Others will say it was just for fashion or a result of a syphilis outbreak leaving a lot of people bald. In any event, it's evident that people often want what they don't have. The only issue with us wanting what we don't have is that we've been programmed to believe that what we have isn't good enough, despite others appropriating our styles.

Some of you will find this loving your hair rule hard to follow and will read it that we can't have protective braided styles and rock wigs to change up our looks because it means we don't love ourselves. Now if that's what it takes for you to fully embrace the hair that grows from your head, then go ahead and throw all that stuff in the trash. But remember that even the ancient Egyptians had their own form of protective wigs that doubled as a symbol of status. So, you can continue to style your hair as you choose, yet it's important to discontinue this narrative that some hair is worse than others simply because it's less straight, courser or doesn't seem to grow as quickly. Our hair grows up and out towards the almighty sun; we must embrace its strength and admire its beauty. Basically, if you are still blessed to have it grow fully from your head, cherish it. It's time to fall in love with what God gave us.

17. Don't use stereotypes to quantify blackness

"The whole idea of a stereotype
is to simplify."
– Chinua Achebe

Description

For over a century, Hollywood has played a major role in creating African-American stereotypes. In the early days of cinema, the black female was always seen as the *Mammy* archetype. Since the early 1990s, the most consistent depiction was that of the *welfare queen* or the *angry black woman*. The black male stereotype has gone through several changes over the years too. Initially starting with the *Stepin Fetchit* character who was lazy and unintelligent, you also had the *magical negro*, both types friendly and palatable to the masses. By the 1970s, the black character in movies had gone from friendly to frightening and would mostly be depicted as a *thug* in some way, shape or form. We'd be remiss to ignore the emergence of the young, black and single professionals that graced America's television programming as well as the upwardly mobile black family sitcoms of the late '80s and '90s. However, Hollywood has been pretty consistent with their ghetto, belligerent, underclass and uneducated portrayal of our image to the world. Oh, I almost forgot they did show the world we sang, danced and played sports to a high level. So, what happens if you're a black female and not angry, what if you're a black male and not a criminal? What if you're an educated black person, not from a ghetto who doesn't play sport and not particularly musical? I'll tell you what happens, you'll have to prove your blackness to every ignorant person you meet.

The Brooklynite

The borough of Brooklyn is where Antoine grew up, in a beautiful brownstone in the heart of Bed-Stuy in the early 1990s. He was born to African-American parents who moved from North Carolina in the 1970s for more opportunities. Upon hearing that, you might have an image of Antoine purely based on the area in which he was born and raised. Although Antoine lived in Bed-Stuy, he didn't spend that much time there as a child because his parents bused him out to school in Suffolk County.

Both Antoine's parents were educated people, his mother a midwife and his father an engineer. Antoine was a big fan of hip hop and attended rap battles in the streets with local would-be rappers. He'd even set up a dance crew with a few of his friends in the area and would enter competitions against rival crews across Brooklyn. Antoine was a good kid. Other than his schoolwork, his main interests were music and dancing right up until he graduated from high school. He attended Tuskegee University where he earned himself a bachelor's degree in aerospace science engineering. As you can imagine, his parents were very proud. With a job lined up working for a company in Lincoln, Antoine was ready to relocate to the state of Nebraska. He moved into a brand new 1100 square foot condominium in the downtown area. Rental prices were considerably cheaper than what he was used to living in New York, so he took full advantage. That wasn't the only thing that was considerably different. It was the polar opposite of home – back there he just blended in, but in Lincoln he stood out like a sore thumb. This didn't concern Antoine though, as he was knowledgeable in the art of code switching, a skill he'd learnt from going to school in Suffolk County. Very quickly into his new career Antoine noticed a recurring theme from his colleagues; upon meeting him, they would finish the conversation by saying, "You're not at all what I thought you'd be like." Although he was curious, Antoine didn't want to rock the boat as he was still new, so he just kept his head down and got on with his work. By now a few years had passed, and he had made close friendships with some of his colleagues. Although there weren't many black people in the town, he did attempt to build relationships with some of the local brothers and sisters. However, it proved to be a difficult task. The ones he encountered all seemed very cliquey, to which Antoine attributed to them having a small town mentality. Nonetheless, he was very settled in his new life: he attended poker nights with the guys from work, frequented the country club and he even took up golf. The only thing that was missing was a woman. He had been so caught up with his career that he just parked the idea of dating.

One Friday night, he was out in a bar with one of his colleagues, Tim, having a few beers. Antoine decided to ask Tim a question that had been on his mind for a long time. He asked Tim why he felt the need to mention about him being different to what he expected when they first spoke. Tim responded, "I just thought that you would be more...black." Although Antoine had an idea of what to expect, he couldn't help being shocked by that response. "What do you mean?" he asked, hoping for some clarification. Tim went on to explain, "I heard you were from Brooklyn and I just thought that you would be intimidating, but you're not at all, you're a really cool guy." The night continued, but what Tim had said played on Antoine's mind that whole evening.

The following Monday, Antoine went into work and was greeted by a wide smile from the new receptionist, Suzan. She immediately caught his attention because she was not just beautiful, but also a sister. He made up his mind then and there that he had to figure out a way of setting up a date. Antoine's game had deteriorated during his time in Lincoln. He always considered himself pretty smooth back in Brooklyn but was moving very slow with Suzan. Each morning he would see her and say hello and she would reply back with a smile. He'd then tell himself that he would speak to her at lunch time. Lunch time would pass without him saying anything. Then, he'd convince himself that he would speak to her at the end of the day. This went on for several weeks. One lunch time, he was speaking to his friend Tim and he told him that he just needed to go over and ask her out. It was exactly what he needed to hear, so at the end of that day he went over to Suzan and asked her if she would like to come out one night after work. Suzan accepted and they agreed to go out on the Friday. They went to a popular bar downtown that served food. The date was going great. After a few drinks, Suzan decided to be more candid with the conversation, "You're not at all how I expected you to be," she said. Antoine wanted to know where she was going with the statement so asked a question, "What do you mean by that?" Suzan paused for a second or two before answering, "Well, it's just that you work as an aviation engineer, I've only ever seen you with white people, and you talk different. Considering all of that, I just didn't expect you to be so black."

The Mixed Race Girl

Atlanta was a great city to grow up in during the early 2000s. The weather was pretty good and southern hospitality was a welcomed staple. Sydney was a thriving eleven year old, living there with her mother, brother and dad. Sydney's mom was black, and her dad was white. Her father had always taught her that she got the best of both worlds: beautiful tanned skin coupled with curls from her mama and big green eyes from her daddy. Sydney felt like she was lucky to be a part of two different cultures, especially since her dad was originally from Italy and often spoke to her in Italian. Her friends never really noticed that her family was different from theirs, until she got to middle school. On the first day, she found herself in unfamiliar territory as most of her friends went on to the neighbouring school.

Middle school can be pretty cutthroat, so she felt she had to make new friends in a hurry and was clearly struggling. Some girls started picking on her by saying things like, "What are you, anyway? Are you actually even black?" She'd respond with, "I'm mixed. My mom is black, and my dad is white." To which she'd typically get some variation of, "Well, you aren't black then. You even talk like a white girl." This kind of questioning of her blackness carried on through much of her middle school years. She was often teased for thinking she had *good hair*, apparently better than her teenaged counterparts born to two black parents. The implication was that she thought she was better than them when all she could think about was how she just wanted to fit in. Girls like these were a common thread in the fabric of her adolescence. They acted as gatekeepers to the full black society that she felt she wasn't granted access to. She eventually found a motley crew of girls to befriend and stuck with them throughout middle school. By the time she got to high school, she was pretty self-assured and didn't allow herself to be put in any racial box or stereotypes. She was just Sydney, not black, not white, not mixed. Just Sydney. All her friends accepted her for simply being herself.

High school was an exciting time filled with different subjects to explore, new responsibilities and eventually baby steps into adulthood. This started with the college admission process. She sat down with her mother and discussed the options. Her mom pushed for her to attend her alma-mater, Spellman. Sydney was reluctant to attend an HBCU as she thought it would just be a whole campus filled with the kind of mean girl treatment she'd experienced throughout her teenaged years. Unwilling to take no for an answer, her mother booked a campus tour the following week. Surprisingly, with her mom's efforts, Sydney fell in love with the place. She was particularly impressed with their psychology department as well as all the extracurricular activities available on site. The icing on the cake was the fact that it wasn't far from home. She loved Atlanta and was happy that she could stay at home and save money on room and board.

That fall, Sydney was off to her first college class. It was completely different to high school; it was more demanding but also liberating. She was in charge of her schedule and even her friendship circle. She didn't feel relegated to the group of girls that didn't seem to fit. Instead, she found most of the girls quite friendly. Over 95% of the girls there were black, but nobody acted like a lot of the black girls at her middle and high school. Nobody questioned what kind of black she was or why her hair grew more quickly downward rather than up and out. Nobody told her she talked *like a white girl*. She started to wonder why the girls back in the day behaved that way. Maybe they just didn't know any better, she thought to herself.

Summary

Though this book is all about rules of blackness, there aren't levels to this. You aren't blacker than your neighbour if you abide by all twenty one. The rules should be used to regain power and pride that colonisation sought to destroy. Blackness isn't a spectrum of varying degrees of strength. You simply are or aren't black, and that is solely based on whether or not you claim some ounce of African ancestry. These rules are meant to strengthen us as a people by increasing mindfulness and positivity into our everyday actions and interactions. One thing that will aid in that endeavour is to not pit each other against one another based on how black (or not) we deem someone to be. Blackness looks and feels different to all of us and we must respect that. What we won't do is be our own brothers' gatekeepers, choosing who we let into the kingdom based on stereotypes that typically lack merit (and most of which we didn't even invent ourselves).

18. Take the teachings to the village

"Education is the most powerful weapon which you can use to change the world."
– Nelson Mandela

Description

In our communities, the most brilliant of us tend to shine and be recognised for their abilities. From a young age, they are identified as gifted and talented and promoted via avenues such as the arts, academics or sports. These individuals find their niche and can be chosen for scholarships or scouted to play for the best college teams. They go on to own their businesses, work for prestigious firms or make universally dope art. They play the best positions on your favourite teams as well. We have proven that we can excel in any field we put our energy towards. Once we hit the height of our game, a lot of us even reconnect with our former community. Yet some of us learn the game and never bring it back to the village.

The Rapper

Senegalese-American Aliaume Damala Badara Akon Thiam was born on 16 April 1973 in St Louis, Missouri, USA. You may know him as Akon. Akon's story actually isn't a cautionary tale. He is the embodiment of how we should always share our knowledge and/or resources with our greater community. Akon co-founded Akon Lighting Africa in 2014 to support Africans in several nations by providing electricity via solar power. Within the charity, there is the Solar Academy in Mali where students are taught the technology necessary to both carry on the teachings of the academy and encouraged to continue to develop further technological advances in the field. Now some people may look at what Akon has done and discredit him by saying that he was just the black face for a Chinese endeavour or that he was not the mastermind and the company was just using his name. Whether there is any truth to those claims, you cannot deny that Akon didn't need to get involved. Akon was likely in a financial position where he could sit back and enjoy his wealth. He could have done what many people do: nothing.

The Billionaire

The Nigerian Billionaire Aliko Dangote donated a building to be used as a business school at Bayero University in Nigeria. Dangote explained that his vision was to drive entrepreneurship education to the highest level in the country. The program became the first business school in Nigeria to offer a PhD in business studies. Mr Dangote said, "My interest for supporting higher education in Nigeria stems from a belief that we can and we should provide the same quality of education here in Nigeria like anywhere else in the world. Good quality education is fundamental in breeding a vibrant economy and society." Aliko didn't want to do what the majority of the charity organisations do when they go to

Africa, such as build a well so that a small village can have clean drinking water. He wanted to give people the opportunity to be able to do what he managed to achieve.

The Game Changers

Richard Theodore Greener was the first African-American to graduate from Harvard university. He went on to do big things like become the Dean of the Howard University School of Law, a General Consul in India and an American representative in the Russo-Japanese war. Arguably, Greener paved the way for the likes of students like the first black US president, Barrack Obama, who went on to attend Harvard after him. People like Greener and Obama are instrumental in showing the world that we too are brilliant if only given the opportunity. Men like these also serve as examples for the rest of us who may think we don't belong somewhere. Both could have retired after becoming the first of their kind in both areas and we'd let them drop the mic.

Summary

Is it enough to just be the first at something? Is it enough to just provide hope by creating a visual for the kids that was previously inconceivable? Maybe. Or have we reached a point where it isn't enough to just pave the way? Could we benefit more from bringing our skinfolk and kinfolk to the path itself and help them along the journey?

We naturally have a more communal approach to life. When you were a kid, I'll bet you were disciplined by aunties, neighbours and family friends. When your blood cousin or even your play-play cousin needs help with her kids, you welcome them into your home as if they are your own, ensuring they meet the same expectations as your own children. When you do well, you want those closest to you to feel your success. Let's face it, it just feels better when you share the wealth, whether that be physical wealth or wealth of knowledge. So, when we learn better and decide to do better for ourselves and our families, we must extend that to our communities. Don't keep those secrets to success to yourself; be the light that you wish someone was to you when all seemed dark and hope was lost. Whatever teachings you have absorbed through life and experience will be greatly appreciated by those who haven't been as fortunate as you. It is your duty to pass that knowledge on to your brothers and sisters.

19. Don't hate on the youth

"It is easier to build strong children
than to repair broken men."
– Frederick Douglass

Description

Kids these days – they don't make it easy for us. Their pants either sag too low or are worn too tight. No one ever knows what they're talking about. And their music isn't even fit for my dog's ears. In fact, every generation is ten times worse than the previous (if you ask the elders). But are they really worse than you were? Or are you being just a little extra? Maybe we could have an ounce more compassion for our youth instead of always knocking them down. Who knows, they might prove worthy of a having a torch or two passed down to them.

The Pound Cake

In 2004, Bill Cosby gave his infamous *pound cake* speech where he made comparisons between the parenting of his day to the parenting of present day. He made some scathing remarks about single mothers. He also criticised the youth for wearing their pants too low and for their inability to grasp the English language. Although his intentions were good, it wasn't well received by the youth who heard it differently from how it was intended to be heard. When Bill Cosby begun his undignified fall from grace, the youth of 2004 were now the adults of 2018. That segment of the community was in their late twenties and early thirties at that time. Once they heard of the accusations, they viewed him as a hypocrite.

Albeit almost fifteen years prior, the *pound cake* speech still left a bitter taste in their mouths and they had little sympathy for the man who was once dubbed America's dad.

The Kid with Big Ideas

Yusef was a young kid with big ideas. Like many of the boys in his neighbourhood, he had dreams of escaping to someplace else. Somewhere you don't hear gunshots and police sirens so frequently that it becomes normal. Yusef could ball at a decent level, but he wasn't delusional. He knew that it wasn't going to get him a college scholarship. Yusef spent nights on YouTube watching videos on people who claimed to have made a million bucks, who claimed to have the secret to success.

One night, he discovered this brother online, who was talking about trading stocks and bonds, explaining how he made a whole year's salary in three months of work. Maybe because it was a brother or maybe because it made sense, either way Yusef decided to buy what he was selling: an online mentor package where he taught you and other paying clients how to make money from the stock market. Yusef used the money that he made from his weekend job at the ice cream shop to fund his new venture. Each day after school, he went through the emails the mentor sent him in meticulous detail. He made notes on each point he wanted more information on. At the end of the week, the group would meet online for two hours and although he was the youngest, Yusef was the one who always had the most pensive questions. That first month Yusef spent every spare moment he had learning as if his life depended on it.

It was a perfect storm – Yusef's logical head, the mentor's good advice and the desire to succeed all assisted in Yusef taking his account from a few hundred dollars to thousands within a few months of trading. He was well on target to achieve what his mentor had said was possible. As sensible as Yusef was he was still a teenager, although eighteen, so he did what anyone his age would do. He bought himself new clothes, sneakers and some jewellery with his hard-earned money.

As the months passed, Yusef was making the money faster than he could spend it. He refurnished the house for his parents, got his dad a new car and treated his siblings to new computers and phones. He even gave money to his two closest friends and mentored them in trading.

Ironically, his Uncle Greg didn't seem too thrilled with his nephew's newfound wealth. Greg lived a few blocks away and was his mother's younger brother. He was around twenty years older than Yusef. "So, I hear you're good on them computers?" asked Uncle

Greg. "Well Uncle, I just use the computer. It's trading that I actually do," replied Yusef. "You think you're smarter than me because you can use a computer?" snapped Uncle Greg. Yusef always had a good relationship with his uncle up to that point. Uncle Greg used to babysit Yusef and the two would play video games and stay up watching superhero movies. He had respect for him as an elder and didn't want to argue so he went into his backpack and took out a large wad of cash and handed it to his uncle. "Take this," said Yusef. This only angered Uncle Greg even more, "Who the hell do you think you are? I remember wiping your backside only yesterday!" His uncle kept the money and stormed out of the house.

Summary

Sometimes our own failures can be amplified when we see a kid half our age achieving the goals that we didn't quite reach. It may feel like they don't show us the respect that we believe is deserved, regardless of whether we have shown them anything to warrant their respect. These children become adults, and they tend to have long memories. If we show them disdain, that will only come back to haunt us.

For it is true that it actually does take a village to raise these youths, our youths. And just as we will take all our teachings to all those in the village, we will embrace all the children as if they were our own. We have a duty to not just chastise the youth when we see them making unwise choices, but to teach them a better way. It's also imperative that we show them respect and hear them out when they have something to say, for some will just write off what they believe as the foolish meanderings of a child. Just think of how many young brothers and sisters who may have been headed down an unsavoury path, yet change direction because an older, wiser mentor showed them a better way — or just took the time to listen to them in a world where they felt voiceless.

20. Support black businesses and sustain intergenerational wealth

"We cannot compete in business unless we unite and get some of this earth so that we can produce our own people's needs."
– Elijah Muhammad

Description

The free market is a multicultural melting pot of innovative designs and funky fashions to pique everyone's interests. We can buy German cars, Italian suits, Indian hair and even frequent the local Vietnamese nail salon for those one-of-a-kind designs. We are free to take our money to any business we deem worthy of our patronage. We are blessed to choose. So why is it we consistently overlook our brothers and sisters when spending our dough?

The Civil War

Most of us know that the USA had a massive Civil War way back in the day. It lasted from 1861-1865, and while the war was fought over a few different things, the main takeaway was that the north wanted to do away with slavery while the south wished to keep all their slaves forever and ever more. Ok, we're all caught up on the basics. Now here's where it gets good. Blacks who lived in the north were enlisted to fight on the side of the union army, the north, and as they were free, they were to be compensated for their services. How awesome is that? Blacks in the north could fight for their country to do away with the enslavement of their own people. In the end, the north won and the USA outlawed slavery as it currently existed, as in you couldn't have people live and tend your land whilst calling you master and not pay them any money for it. All was well. Everyone was happy, well, everyone except the salty south because now their labour force was no longer free. Anyway, these newly freed folks needed some help in navigating the system the colonists had previously set up for themselves. At the end of the war, the US Congress set up the Freedmen's Bureau, with the architects envisioning a one-stop shop for all the social servicing needs of African-Americans. With its inception, included other services like the Freedmen's Saving Bank.

Money deposited in this bank came from various sources of income such as soldiers employed by the army and those who worked for the organisation. The bank's branches were springing up across the country. It was indeed symbolic as a promise for hope in the negro dream converging with the American dream. African-Americans were contributing to the economy on a larger scale, many owning their own properties too. Unfortunately, the bank was short-lived, and congress ultimately decided to close up shop. They cited the reasons for the bank's failure to be a combo of inexperience by those working at the ground level, coupled with the national economy declining in 1873. Another reason mentioned was how American financier and bank board member Henry Cooke may have inappropriately used some of its assets and funnelled them into his own family's banking business. Millions of dollars were initially lost by bank account holders (keep in mind that millions of dollars back then went even further than it would today), only to have a fraction of those losses recouped years later.

The Hustler

Cleon once was a hustler from the mid 1980s to the late 1990s in Chicago. He bragged that he could sometimes make the same in one day that a waiter would make in a whole year. He had all the spoils that came with that particular lifestyle – the pretty girls, fancy cars, nice jewellery and expensive clothes. Cleon was well known in his neighbourhood and very much respected. At the height of his pomp, Cleon had a luxury British automobile and lived in a penthouse. In Cleon's line of work the reward was sometimes big, but the risk was always huge. He had a real good run of success and flirted with the idea of getting out of the game, but he loved the admiration and status just as much as he loved the money.

By the late 1990s, Cleon experienced an occupational hazard which resulted in him serving twenty years in a correctional facility. All Cleon's big ticket items had been seized and the money that he had stashed away was periodically absorbed by baby mommas, girlfriends and family members. Upon release Cleon was stone broke, not a penny to his name. During his incarceration Cleon found God and became very religious. He repented for his sins and rejected his previous life; he was a reformed character. He planned to give something back to the community, ideally by speaking about the illusions of his past life. He wanted to share his story, of how there are no happy endings. Cleon intended to catch the youth early so they could learn from his mistakes. He had moved into his sister's small apartment and began working on how he could speak at youth centres and high schools to really make a difference. That same evening Cleon was visited by the eldest of his three children whom he had not seen since he was seven, Rob. They embraced and Rob gave him a rundown of Cleon's other two children. Richie was locked up for robbery and doing ten years, but Kelly had moved down south and was doing well. Rob then went on to talk about his business venture – he was a bit of an entrepreneur. He started a tech company the previous year but needed a little investment to take the business to the next level. Cleon picked up his duffle bag and was fumbling around inside, he then took out a bible and placed it into his son's hand, "Son, I'd love to support your business, but this is the only thing that I can give you right now."

The Sandwich Shop

As Karl and Gavin stepped out for their lunch break, Gavin went to go into the new sandwich shop across the street, "I heard a brother owns that place over there, let's go check it out." Karl started walking in the opposite direction toward the burger van. "Where you going?" asked Gavin.

"I went there last week, and he got my order wrong, I wanted BBQ sauce and he gave me ketchup, so I'm not going there again. He's lost my business," replied Karl. Gavin paused for a moment before he answered, "You've been going to the burger van for over a year and you complain every time, but you keep going back, so what's the difference?"

Summary

Alright, so there's blatantly a large gap in wealth when one examines the black diaspora versus the white population, especially in the USA. We just aren't sustaining intergenerational wealth at the same rate as our white counterparts. Some would say we're just slacking and need to pull ourselves up by our bootstraps, right? But let's not forget the efforts made by African-Americans to accumulate wealth, plans that arguably have been thwarted at every turn. Our lives in the Americas started with 246 years of slavery. Then we were free and had our money mismanaged by the Freedman's Bureau. Also, we had our very own Black Wall Street that in 1921 was massacred. Oh yeah, and the Jim Crow Era's Black Codes set a host of discriminatory practices that had long lasting effects throughout the twentieth century (and beyond). Black folks in the USA ain't had it easy. And even though other countries that house the diaspora have practised more sophisticated versions of racism (we're looking at you, Great Britain), our peoples still only seem to be on the cusp of where we ultimately need to be financially. Because of this, we must press on. Black folks all over must press on. We have the ability to set up future generations, but it must start today. Invest in each other. Invest in us.

21. Never apologise for your blackness

"My name is Jack Johnson. I'm the heavyweight champion of the world. I'm black. They never let me forget it. I'm black alright. I'll never let them forget it."
– Jack Johnson

Description

Whether it be hair, music, food or fashion sense, there are definite things which separate us from our white counterparts. These things can be deemed black, sometimes creating curiosity, unwanted attention or even offence. In order to deal with these possibilities, we sometimes tone down appearance and mute our actions as a way of making our Caucasian brethren feel more comfortable. Oddly enough in our desperation to put the European at ease, history shows us that we have never been granted the same courtesy.

The ATM

Although it was only a little after five o'clock, it was already very dark as that December chill was cutting through the air. Carnell had just finished work, so he was in his cashmere winter coat with his blue shirt and yellow tie very visible. He was on his way to meet a few friends for drinks at a bar which wasn't too far from his office building. As he walked down the street, a middle-aged white lady had just finished using an ATM machine. She looked over at Carnell very sheepishly and continued walking in front of him down the same street. Carnell noticed that she was holding her handbag very tightly and that she was moving very quickly. He came to the conclusion that he must have been making her uneasy as she made a cash withdrawal and was paranoid that he was walking directly behind her. Carnell was a very mindful guy, so he decided to continue his journey from across the street to put the woman at ease. The woman carried on but kept looking over her shoulder from the other side of the road whilst clutching her bag against her chest. Carnell could see the woman was in distress so sped up in order to be in front of her so that she would then realise that he was not following her.

The bar was across the street, so Carnell had to cross back over the road. As he crossed the road, the woman started screaming for the police even though he was about ten yards in front of her. Carnell rushed over to the woman and started to reassure her that he was not a mugger. He told her that he had just finished work and was heading to the bar right on that corner. The woman was visibly shaken up, but

Carnell was able to eventually calm her down and she was able to walk to her car. When Carnell finally arrived at the bar his friend was waiting outside. "What was that foolish behaviour I just saw?" asked his friend. Carnell answered the question, "Oh, the lady thought I was a mugger and freaked out, she calmed down, once I explained everything though." His friend then responded, "I was actually referring to your behaviour."

The Barber's Chair

As Joel sat patiently waiting to be called up, he kept playing with his dreadlocks that he had been growing since his senior year of high school. He would take a lock and twiddle it around his finger just like he often did throughout college, usually when he was concentrating.

The barber, sporting a recently lined up afro and taped beard, signalled Joel that he was ready for him. The moment of truth had arrived, and Joel reluctantly sat down in the chair. "What you having, brother?" the barber asked. Joel replied, "Take it all off." As the barber was adjusting the chair he asked, "Why you taking all this off?"

Joel responded, "Well, I've just finished college and I will be going for interviews and I just need to make sure I look professional, you know what I mean?" The barber's face stayed completely emotionless as he replied, "No brother, I don't know what you mean at all."

The Black Man's New Clothes

Upon returning from his vacation in the Gambia, Desmond had a suitcase full of new clothes. He absolutely fell in love with the style and culture of the small West African country. His wife, who was no different, had many garments made to her specifications while she was there too. Desmond's business partner Stuart had invited him to a party the weekend he got back; it was a baby shower for one of their clients.

The venue was outdoors in a quaint little country pub twenty miles south of London. Stuart agreed to collect Desmond so they could travel down in one car. The two of them had been friends for many years before eventually going into business together. They ran a successful recruitment agency and it was always good practice to attend the events of their clients to provide that personal touch. Stuart arrived to collect Desmond and was shocked to see Desmond dressed in an African dashiki two piece suit. "Is that what you're wearing?" asked Stuart.

"Yes, why?" replied Desmond. Stuart looked Desmond up and down, "Nobody else is going to be wearing anything like that," he said. Desmond smiled and then replied, "That's exactly why I am wearing it."

Summary

Did Kobe Bryant apologise for being one of the best basketball players of all time with his ability to shoot winning shots at the end of nail-biting NBA games? Did Serena Williams apologise for revolutionising the way we look at women's tennis? Did Mary Seacole apologise for being a better Florence Nightingale than Nightingale herself? Did George Washington Carver apologise for being so darn innovative with those peanuts? Probably not. They were unapologetically pioneering in their chosen fields, representing beacons of excellence for all of us spectators. We need to associate this level of excellence with blackness. We are capable of great things and need not dim our lights, quieten our voices or be humble in our accomplishments. Set your black dial to full peacock mode at all times, exhibiting unwavering pride to any and everyone who crosses your path. For if it offends, the issue is not with you but with the one who is offended. Be you, be unapologetically black.

Conclusion

How you feeling? Good, we hope. Extra black, even? Ideally, this lovely little compact guide to greatness has resonated with you and yours, reminding you of what we can be if only we stay committed to ourselves. Throughout the world, they will try to tell you what it means to be black. They'll have us believe that we aren't good enough, that little old ladies should fear our sons, that our daughters are not beautiful, that our fathers don't care. In the hearts and minds of the wise, we'll know it's a load of nonsense and treat it as such. But what about those who are impressionable?

While there are plenty of non-black allies around, the media will do their best to plague the minds of the ignorant. They will guide the narrative of a newsworthy story by using language to either vilify or dignify the characters. Take for instance how a young white murderer may be given a headline that begins with *Suspected gunman and formerly bullied teen...* Compare this to that of a young black man who was murdered (without proper cause) by the police whose headline might make mention of that fact that he had ...*traces of marijuana in his system at the time of his death.* All too often we see the white character's highlight reel publicised (even when they've done wrong) whilst we have our lowest moments made public, including any family members with a remotely objectionable past. We then have to enter conversations with people (of all races) who are already biased about who's right and wrong in a particular situation because the facts no longer matter. The image we are given by the media becomes our opinion of the actors in the event. Now for the most part, we can differentiate between what is fact and fiction, but every now and again one of us struggles to understand how the media plays us.

The onus is on us, guys. We are our own brothers' keepers. In order to combat the hate, we must double up on the love: love for ourselves and everything black. The time has come to give our black businesses a go instead of criticising their perceived imperfections. It's time to embrace the skin, hair and bodies that were gifted to us, that we rightfully deserve. It's time to praise each other in public and know that one sister's success is a success for us all. It's time to be deliberate in our positions of pro blackness to anyone who questions it. It's time to toss away colonial notions of yester-year with a confident knowingness that no one can take away. It's time to recognise our infinite worth as a collective of talented minds and take what is for us. It's time to take all of these teachings to anyone who needs to learn them.

It will be easier for some to get on board than it will be for others, and that's ok. We're all aiming to live our best black lives – to be the most perfect version of ourselves. Nonetheless, it's a journey to get there. Even the brilliant scholars, poets and revolutionaries quoted in this book haven't followed all twenty one rules religiously. Though now you've got these parables of triumph and cautionary tales to draw from, it should be easy to see how important these rules are for all of us. As Marcus Garvey so eloquently put it, "If we as a people realised the greatness from which we came, we would be less likely to disrespect ourselves." Let's respect ourselves so much that we start to follow as many of these rules as possible. Self-improvement may seem an onerous task, but this task is very achievable and necessary. Let us get on code and hold ourselves to a high standard, without pointing fingers at those who fall short. Instead, we will set the example for others to follow.

21 Rules of Blackness Checklist

1. ☐ Know your worth
2. ☐ Don't force yourself on people
3. ☐ Never underestimate yourself
4. ☐ Build on your physical advantages
5. ☐ Don't be a victim
6. ☐ Eat foods intended for melanin rich people
7. ☐ Acknowledge your connection to Africa
8. ☐ Don't sit on the fence
9. ☐ Never change teams
10. ☐ Always celebrate our successes
11. ☐ Never speak negatively of black people in front of non-black people
12. ☐ Choose the right partner
13. ☐ Be an ambassador at all times

14	☐	Never make excuses for racist behaviour
15	☐	Discontinue the use of colonial belief systems
16	☐	Love your hair
17	☐	Don't use stereotypes to quantify blackness
18	☐	Take the teachings to the village
19	☐	Don't hate on the youth
20	☐	Support black business & sustain intergenerational wealth
21	☐	Never apologise for your blackness

Made in United States
Orlando, FL
26 August 2024